SELECTED WRITINGS OF
ST. THOMAS AQUINAS

The Principles of Nature
On Being and Essence
On the Virtues in General
On Free Choice

Translated, with introductions and notes, by

Robert P. Goodwin

D0974634

Bobbs-Merrill Educational Publishing
Indianapolis

Nihil Obstat: Richard T. Wurzel, S.T.D. Censor Deputatus
Imprimatur: George J. Rehring, S.T.D. Bishop of
     Toledo, Ohio *September 8, 1965*
The *Nihil Obstat* and *Imprimatur* are official declarations
that a book or pamphlet is free of doctrinal or moral error.
No implication is contained therein that those who have
granted the *Nihil Obstat* and *Imprimatur* agree with the
contents, opinions, or statements expressed.

The Bobbs-Merrill Company,
4300 West 62nd Street
Indianapolis, Indiana 46268

First Edition
Eleventh Printing—1981

Library of Congress Catalog Card Number: 65–26529
ISBN 0–672–60469–8 (pbk)

For Elaine

Contents

General Introduction

Contemporary students of philosophy are frequently hesitant or reluctant to study the areas of medieval thought. Although they occasionally hear that there was some philosophical speculation during the Middle Ages, a superficial perusal of its literature leads many to conclude that medieval thought was exclusively theological. Their reaction is either to close the book, or to conclude that medieval philosophy is of such an odd sort that it is unworthy of genuine philosophical analysis. This volume is designed to show that during the Middle Ages, especially in the writings of St. Thomas Aquinas, real philosophical speculation did occur and, hence, merits the type of analysis usually accorded such speculation.

Aquinas was Italian by birth. Scholars differ on his year of birth, either 1224 or 1225. At the age of five he was placed by his parents in the famous Benedictine monastery of Monte Cassino. At nine he commenced his studies of the arts and philosophy at the University of Naples; at approximately twenty-five years of age, he began what we might call graduate studies in the then young University of Paris. Four years later he became a master, that is, an accepted member of the theological faculty at Paris. The rest of his academic life was spent in Paris and in Italy, doing both teaching and extensive writing. He died in 1275. While biographical highlights are fairly easy to establish, the interpretation of his writings is a matter of continuous concern.

Every student of philosophy realizes that in order to grasp the meaning of any philosopher's writings, he must be aware of the philosopher's cultural and intellectual environment. This is especially true of the medieval philosophers, whose milieu was so different from ours. It is not possible in this introduction to make an extensive review of the intellectual and cultural environment of the thirteenth century, but certain relevant circumstances can be isolated and described which ought to make the philosophical speculation of Aquinas more intelligible to the contemporary student. Moreover, it should tend to make Aquinas' views more approachable, and less odd than they might appear at first acquaintance.

There is one further advantage for the student in knowing the historical background: occasionally the historical circumstances within which a philosopher does his contemplation are extremely conducive to profound and lasting insights which would be missed or overlooked in some other age. The knowledge of these circumstances becomes absolutely necessary, therefore, for capturing the full significance of such insights. On the other hand, to set a philosophy within a context is sometimes misleading. It might very well (as has happened) tend to give the reader the impression that what a man has said at one point in history is really relevant only for that time. No such historicism is intended here. Yet the function of history in relation to a philosophical doctrine is itself a philosophical problem, which must ultimately be left for the student of philosophy to speculate upon.

However one may feel about the problem of historicism, three historical factors must be analyzed if St. Thomas is to be understood: first, the philosophical aim; second, the discovery of Aristotle; and third, the mode of composing treatises.

It is, and perhaps always will be, a matter of scholarly debate to what extent the religion of a period or of a philosopher himself influences directly or indirectly, positively or negatively, any single man's philosophical speculation during a given period. Names like Plato, Descartes, Kant, for example, never seem to be able to be completely disengaged from some kind of religion. What is said, however, of these and so many other philosophers is especially true of the medieval intellectuals, whose intentions and aims were patently religious. From Augustine in the fifth century to the commentators of the Renaissance, philosophical speculation was for theological ends. These men were operating under the dictum "faith seeking understanding." Except for the Moslems, these men were Christians and attempted to achieve intellectual understanding of that to which they had given religious commitment.

The teachings of Jesus Christ were at once profound and paradoxically simple. Christ did not address Himself to intellectuals; His intention was to bring a message of salvation to all men—the unlearned and the learned, the rich and the poor, the sick and the healthy. Almost from the beginning of Christianity, however, some men attempted intellectually to penetrate and analyze the Christian message, and to ask that fundamental question—*Why?*—of all its phases. Christ did not teach a metaphysics, epistemology, or ethics. But what He did teach stimulated the intellectually inclined to speculate about the nature of reality, of knowledge, of the good, and of the beautiful. In short, some men found that a philosophical approach was necessary to their intellectual appreciation of the good news of Christianity. These men were the theologians, and it is for this reason that they are sometimes called philosophers, and at other times Christian philosophers.

Perhaps some examples might help. The medieval Christians believed that Adam's sin in some way damaged him and all men who came after him. It damaged them as men. They also believed that Christ's redemptive act made a repair possible—made it possible, in fact, to live a better life than could be lived by a man in a purely natural state. For a man who is not intellectually inclined, for a man simply seeking salvation, this is indeed good news. It is good news for the intellectual, too, but for him it is also an occasion for inquiry, stimulating him to ask, *What is this human nature damaged by original sin? In what could this damage consist?* Now to speculate about human nature is to philosophize, and whether they are called philosophers or theologians who philosophized, these men did ask many of the questions raised by Plato, Aristotle, and many other philosophers whose aims were not specifically theological.

One more example. Christ indeed taught a moral doctrine,

the heart of which was love, but He never submitted this relationship to philosophical analysis. Moreover, He preached a superior kind of love, a supernatural love. To understand this, however, the Christian philosophers felt the need of first analyzing and describing love in a natural sense; only then did they attempt to develop some notions about the sort of love to which Christ was referring. Again the Christian intellectual had to philosophize; but the point here is not so much what he did, as why. The particular historical circumstances in which he found himself gave his philosophical speculation a goal, the understanding of Christianity.

A certain corollary follows from all of this, and may be of help to the contemporary student of philosophy who is attempting to understand Aquinas. The objective character of St. Thomas' philosophical speculation has been referred to. Apart from contemporary anti-metaphysical philosophy and linguistic analysis, which maintain that philosophers really cannot go any further in their understanding of things than does the ordinary man using only ordinary language, contemporary philosophical speculation adopts quite a different perspective than that of the thirteenth-century scholars. The contemporary thinker philosophizes by attempting to understand himself and those things other than himself in relation to himself. Contemporary thought is oriented toward the personal: the most usual question one finds in contemporary philosophy is, "What is this in relation to me?" This was not true of the medieval thinkers. Basically they were all theologians, and their attempts at speculation consisted in understanding the object of speculation in relation to God. In other words, when the medieval man speculated about human nature he attempted to understand it, but felt that to understand it properly it must be understood in relationship to God. Moreover, the occasions for speculation about human nature in the Middle Ages were primarily the Christian doctrines of creation and of original sin. Now creation is an act of God, and original sin an act directly related to God. Hence, to speculate about human nature was, for these men, to attempt to see it in its relationship to the Divine.

This adopted perspective of the medieval thinkers is perhaps one of the explanations for the occasional coolness with which medieval thought is received by contemporary students of philosophy, and leaves us with another question which must ultimately be left to the reader, that is, whether or not such objective speculation on the part of medieval thinkers can be meaningful for the student of philosophy today.

This discussion of the relationship between theology and philosophy for the men of the Middle Ages leads naturally to the second factor which must be isolated and described, namely, the medieval scholars' discovery of the works of Aristotle. Aristotle, of course, lived during the fourth century B.C. Over the centuries his writings became lost to Western civilization, and it was not until the latter part of the twelfth century and the early part of the thirteenth that the Christians became aware of them. The Moslems, from about the ninth century on, knew Aristotle in both of their intellectual centers: Bagdad in the East and Cordova, Spain, in the West; and it was largely through the contacts between the Arabs and the Christians in Spain that the latter became heir to the Aristotelian corpus.

It is rather difficult for us today to appreciate the significance of this discovery. Perhaps it can be compared to the publication of some of Karl Marx's writings, which, although they did not have a profound effect immediately, in time became veritably earth-shaking for the Western world. Something similar to this occurred within the intellectual community during the thirteenth century. In fact, the discovery of Aristotle by the medieval scholars can be considered one of the major events in Western intellectual history. Aristotle was, and still is, important for anyone seriously interested in philosophy. But the discovery of his works shook the thirteenth-century Christian theologians to their toes. St. Thomas Aquinas can be appreciated only in this light.

It has already been said that the theologian needs a philosophical context within which to carry on his proper activity. From the beginning of Christianity to that pivotal thirteenth century, the only philosophical context available to the Christian theologians was Platonism. Men like St. Augustine, St. Anselm, John Scotus Erigena all placed their theology within a Platonic context. Now Aristotle, as even the beginning student knows, is quite different from Plato. Whereas Plato seems a man with his head in the clouds, Aristotle's feet are firmly planted on the ground. The orientation, spirit, and perspective of Aristotle are quite different from Plato's, as became evident to Aristotle's new discoverers. The aim of these thirteenth-century men was precisely the same as their Christian predecessors, that is, faith seeking understanding. But now a new tool to accomplish this task was at hand. There was, however, one immediate and grave problem. Over the centuries Platonism had become so firmly imbedded in Christian thought that it was practically indistinguishable from Christian dogma. Consequently, the acceptance of Aristotle—or, for a time, even the study of Aristotle—appeared to some as bordering on heresy. This problem gave rise to a tremendous intellectual ferment that began about 1240 and lasted approximately to the end of the century. The issue was whether Aristotle could be an adequate instrument for Christian theology.

The young Aquinas arrived at the University of Paris around 1250. The controversy was still very intense. As far as we know, Aquinas, still only a "graduate student," became immediately involved; in fact, judging from his writing of the period, he became one of the leading mavericks. He was convinced that Aristotle could be used by a Christian theologian, provided there were limitations. There were points within Aristotelian doctrine which were totally unacceptable to any Christian—for example, Aristotle rejected a doctrine of personal immortality, nor could he maintain a doctrine of creation. But Aquinas did find large portions of Aristotelian doctrine useful.

His procedure was not that of simply isolating, adapting, and incorporating various propositions and doctrines. Even at this early date in his academic career, Aquinas was developing his own peculiar metaphysical insight. Under the influence of some earlier thinkers, especially the Arabian Avicenna (980—1037) and William of Auvergne (1180—1249), and under the suggestion of God's "description" of Himself—"I am who am" (Exodus 3:14)—St. Thomas contended that the key factor of any reality as a reality was its existence. Now it is fairly obvious that if anything is real, it must exist. But Aquinas meant more than this. He maintained, or at this time began to maintain, that existence is not simply being present, but rather a constitutive principle possessed by everything real. For him every being possesses a real principle in virtue of which it is. By contrast to so many others, St. Thomas maintained that a being is not a being in virtue of its matter, or a being in virtue of what it is, that is, its essence. The principle in virtue of which something is a being was called *esse,* the act of existing.

A close reading of St. Thomas reveals this insight permeating the whole of his thought. His developing theology reveals this context. Hence, while Aristotle did constitute for Aquinas a major prop on which the latter could lean, that prop was substantially altered under his pervasive metaphysical intuition. What was formerly and formally Aristotelian became Thomistic.[1] On this basis, then, one must maintain at least that Thomas, the theologian, philosophized.

The third factor upon which introductory comments should be made is the mode of composition of theological treatises

---

[1]Parenthetically, it is interesting to note that only now in our day is Christianity searching for a new medium for its theology. The use of Aristotle in the thirteenth century was revolutionary. Furthermore, Aristotle has been for post-thirteenth century theologians what Plato was for pre-thirteenth century theologians. Today, however, for many in both Protestant and Catholic theological circles, the Aristotelian perspective is outmoded. The entrenchment of Aristotle, for which St. Thomas was largely responsible, is itself being besieged. The search seems to be for a new medium.

in the thirteenth century. Upon opening a book composed by St. Thomas or any of the other theologians of the thirteenth century the contemporary student is usually surprised and somewhat repelled by the manner of composition of these works. We are accustomed to finding philosophers composing their works in what might be called ordinary paragraph form —that is, sentence following sentence, paragraph following paragraph, with each paragraph having a central idea or argument and perhaps one central idea pervading the whole of the work in question. Not so with the works of the medieval theologians. What one discovers there is usually a series of what are called questions, articles, and distinctions. First a question is stated, then a series of opinions offered; this is followed by the author's resolution of the problem. The third part of the article consists of comments or replies to the objections or opinions which were raised in the first part of the article. With completion of this article the author begins a second question, using the same format followed in the first. This mode of composition does not usually prick the interest of the reader. Again, however, one must refer to the historical context in which these authors operated, which gives us a logical explanation for this particular style.

The thirteenth-century theological authors whose works are extant were mostly teachers, either at the University of Paris or at Oxford University in England. These teachers, or masters, taught largely by depending upon the opinions of the authors who preceded them. Moreover, these opinions were used dialectically; the master would raise a question, the various known opinions on that question were brought forth and considered, and the master then offered his own view on the question, including the evidence to support his view. This, in turn, was followed by a reconsideration of the opinions of the previous authors, with comments on their views added in the light of the master's position on the problem. On certain occasions during the scholastic year the master would conduct what was called a *disputatio*. This was, in a certain sense, a form of debate carried on by the students. On these occasions it would be the task of the students to cull the opinions of the masters of the past and debate the issues. At the end of the debate the master came forth and presented his resolution of the problem, in the light of what had been said by the past masters, and in the light of his own evidence and reasons. He would also return to the opinions of the past masters and either offer his reasons for disagreeing with them or show how they had been misinterpreted and could be better interpreted in the light of his own opinion.

Now the thirteenth-century theological and philosophical material that we possess today consists for the most part of edited résumés of these discussions that took place in the medieval classroom. This explains the rather extreme structured character of the literature from that period. The last two units in this volume, namely, *On the Virtues in General* and *On Free Choice,* are illustrations of this type of literature. I have deemed it more helpful to the student to omit the first and third section of the articles—that is, the opinions of the past masters, and St. Thomas' answers to them. What is left, then, is the second section, or what is called the body of the article, which related Aquinas' own views along with his evidence. The reader will note that even within the bodies of these articles St. Thomas does take up some of the more serious objections which might be raised on the part of past masters to his own opinion, and attempts to resolve the difficulties involved.

There are some notable exceptions to this rule about the genre of thirteenth-century theological literature. Two of these exceptions are included within this volume. The first two units, *The Principles of Nature* and *On Being and Essence,* are not summaries of debates carried on within the classroom. They are what we might call today monographs, certain rather short treatises written on specific subjects in a non-dialectical way. Each of these units appears to have been written by St. Thomas to elucidate certain philosophical issues for some of his confrères within the academic community. There is a noticeable lack of purely theological material in each of these treatises, which is not the case with the latter two units. It should be remembered, however, that even with these two purely philosophical treatises, St. Thomas' intention was to create an incisive philosophical tool for theological speculation.

As regards the translation itself, I have attempted to render the Latin as meaningful to the contemporary mind as possible. Occasionally this has meant using English terminology which is non-traditional in translating Aquinas. I feel, however, that intelligibility and meaning are more important in translation than frozen traditional terminology.

I cannot close without thanking some of my colleagues and friends who have helped to make this translation possible. Professors John Fitzgibbons of St. Ambrose College, Thomas McTighe of Georgetown University, Joseph Price of Bowling Green State University, and Lucia and Ewing Chinn, all have made very helpful comments and criticisms. I also want to thank some of my students for their help in proofreading, and finally my wife, Elaine, who generously gave her time and energy to typing this manuscript.

Selected Bibliography

Works by St. Thomas Aquinas

Latin Texts From Which the Present Translations Were Made

De Principiis Naturae. Edited by JOHN J. PAUSON. Fribourg: Société Philosophique, 1950.

De Ente et Essentia. Edited by M.-D. ROLAND-GOSSELIN, O.P. Paris: Librairie Philosophique J. Vrin, 1926.

De Virtutibus in Communi, in *Quaestiones Disputatae.* Edited by R. M. SPIAZZI, O.P. 2 vols. Rome-Turin: Marietti, 1954.

De Veritate, in *Quaestiones Disputatae.* Edited by R. M. SPIAZZI, O.P. 2 vols. Rome-Turin: Marietti, 1954.

Complete Works

Opera Omnia. Edited by FRETTÉ and MARÉ. 34 vols. Paris: Vivès, 1871-1880.

Opera Omnia. Leonine edn. 16 vols. to date. Rome, 1882–.

Some English Translations

Basic Writings of Saint Thomas Aquinas. Translated by ANTON C. PEGIS. 2 vols. New York: Random House, 1944.

Commentary on Aristotle's De Anima. Translated by F. K. FOSTER and S. HUMPHRIES. New Haven: Yale University Press, 1951.

Commentary on Aristotle's Physics. Translated by R. J. BLACKWELL, *et al.* New Haven: Yale University Press, 1963.

Commentary on the Metaphysics of Aristotle. Translated by JOHN P. ROWAN. Chicago: H. Regnery, 1961.

On the Truth of the Catholic Faith (Summa Contra Gentiles). Translated by ANTON C. PEGIS, JAMES ANDERSON, VERNON J. BOURKE, CHARLES J. O'NEIL. 5 vols. Garden City: Hanover House, 1954-1956.

Truth. Translated and edited by ROBERT W. SCHMIDT, S.J. 3 vols. Chicago: H. Regnery, 1954.

Secondary Reading

General Histories of the Period

COPLESTON, FREDERICK. *A History of Philosophy.* Vol. II. Westminster, Maryland: Newman Press, 1952.

GILSON, ÉTIENNE. *History of Christian Philosophy in the Middle Ages.* New York: Random House, 1954.

KNOWLES, DAVID. *The Evolution of Medieval Thought.* New York: Vintage Books, 1962.

LEFF, GORDON. *Medieval Thought.* Baltimore: Penguin Books, 1958.

MAURER, ARMAND. *Medieval Philosophy.* New York: Random House, 1962.

PIEPER, JOSEF. *Scholasticism.* New York: Pantheon, 1960.

VIGNAUX, PAUL. *Philosophy in the Middle Ages: An Introduction.* New York: Meridian Books, 1959.

WEINBERG, JULIUS. *A Short History of Medieval Philosophy.* Princeton: Princeton University Press, 1964.

Doctrinal Surveys

COPLESTON, FREDERICK. *Aquinas.* Baltimore: Penguin Books, 1955.

CHENU, M.-D. *Toward Understanding St. Thomas.* Chicago: H. Regnery, 1964.

D'ARCY, MARTIN C. *Thomas Aquinas.* London, 1931.

GILSON, ÉTIENNE. *Christian Philosophy of St. Thomas Aquinas,* Translated by L. K. Shook. New York: Random House, 1956.

———. *Elements of Christian Philosophy.* Garden City: Doubleday, 1960.

SERTILLANGES, A. D. *The Foundations of Thomistic Philosophy.* Translated by G. Anstruther. St. Louis: B. Herder, 1931.

Biographical Studies

CHESTERTON, G. K. *St. Thomas Aquinas.* Garden City: Doubleday, 1936.

FOSTER, KENELEN (ed.). *Life of St. Thomas Aquinas.* New York: Helicon, 1959.

MARITAIN, JACQUES. *St. Thomas Aquinas.* New York: Meridian Books, 1952.

Bibliographical Aids

BOURKE, VERNON. *Thomistic Bibliography, 1920-1940.* St. Louis: St. Louis University Press, 1945.

Bulletin Thomiste. Montréal: Institute d'études médiévales.

MANDONNET, P. and DESTREZ, J. *Bibliographie Thomiste.* Paris: Kain, 1921.

SCHÜTZ, L. *Thomas Lexicon.* 2nd edn. Paderborn, 1895.

The Principles of Nature

Introduction to
The Principles of Nature

The Principles of Nature is an excellent illustration of Aquinas' elucidation and summary of certain Aristotelian ideas which could be of use to a theologian. Specifically, the treatise deals with Aristotle's traditional four causes. It is rather difficult to speak of these four causes today, for the term "cause" has undergone such vigorous analysis since his time, and its meaning has been so drastically modified. Today the meaning of the term even differs from philosopher to philosopher. To many the analysis by David Hume (1711-1776), the British empiricist, was so devastating that the only possible meaning left for the term "cause" was anything immediately preceding an event, or anything without which an event does not occur. To illustrate quite briefly, A is observed invariably to precede event B. Accordingly, A is a cause of B, with "cause" meaning an invariable predecessor of B, or something without which B does not occur. The theory hinges on the empiricism that is brought to the analysis of the term. Note the phrase "is observed" in the above sentence; cause can have meaning only in terms of some kind of sensory experience.

Aristotle was not an empiricist; hence his analysis of causality is quite different from the Humean-inspired one outlined above. To know anything in a scientific way, for Aristotle, is to know it in its causes. A cause, though, is understood as anything which makes a positive contribution to some event. Hume had emphasized simply succession (B follows A); the Stagirite notes the influence of one thing upon another. Hume allows only sensory experience to be relevant to causal events; Aristotle maintains that the human

3

intellect is capable of penetrating an event and discovering genuine influence, which, of course, cannot be grasped in a sensory way.

Maintaining the intellect's ability to grasp what the senses are incapable of grasping, Aristotle continues his analysis of causality and divides causes into four basic kinds: material, formal, moving, and final. The best way of introducing the student to these divisions is perhaps to describe an event and isolate the factors that make a positive contribution to it. Let us use the same illustration used by Aristotle himself: the coming into being of a bronze statue, let us say, of Socrates. Certainly the statue of Socrates would not be what it is coming to be, were it not for the bronze. Hence, the bronze makes a definite contribution to the reality of the statue, and is therefore a cause. Moreover, the shape which is given to the bronze likewise makes a definite contribution to the statue's reality. It would not be a statue of Socrates were it not for the shape imposed upon it. In any event something undergoes some kind of modification. The recipient of the modification is called the material cause, whereas the modification itself is called the formal cause. In addition to the material and formal cause, the statue would not come into being without a sculptor; for that matter, no change would ever occur without something to produce the change. This is referred to as the moving cause. Finally, there is the end or aim of the sculptor. The statue would not be the reality that it is coming to be, were the sculptor not "moved" to sculpt. Let us assume money motivates him. Hence, the conceived money "moves" the man to produce the change in the bronze and, hence, makes a positive contribution to the production of the statue. This end or aim is called the final cause. Accordingly, to know what a thing is being made out of, what is happening to the thing to make it specifically what it is, who or what is changing it, and why the change is being made, is to know the object scientifically or, more simply, causally.

A reading of this treatise reveals some fine distinctions which have to be made within each grouping, and also some other kinds of cause. But the above-mentioned four are the most fundamental, and are accurately defined and described by St. Thomas. It should be noticed, however, that the doctrine of the four causes expounded by Aquinas is definitely colored by his peculiar metaphysical position. As the early part of this treatise shows, the four causes of any being cannot really be understood in St. Thomas's terms unless one sees them in the light of his doctrine of being. The ultimate basic constituent of any being, that is, that which makes a being a being, is what in Latin is designated *esse,* and translated into English as the act of existing. For Aristotle to be a being is to be either a substance or an accident. A substance is anything which exists in itself and not in another, whereas an accident is that which must exist in another—that is, in a substance. This man, that dog, that tree are examples of substances. Color, weight, shape, relations are examples of accidents. Moreover, the real object of the study of being, traditionally metaphysics, is substance—inasmuch as accidents are only affections of substances and, therefore, only secondary. In analyzing substance, Aristotle maintains that it is composed of form and matter. By virtue of the former principle, the substance is what it is, and the latter principle is simply the recipient of the form. Hence, the form *horse* is what makes Seabiscuit of the nature *horse,* whereas its matter is what is modified by this form. The form, then, is that which make Seabiscuit actual, and, incidentally, active. Ultimately the form makes a being a being. Not so with St. Thomas. He retains form, matter, and accidents, but adds what he contends to be the principle in virtue of which a being is a being: the act of existing. Form, for Aristotle, is the supreme actuality; the act of existing plays this role for Aquinas. These are two different metaphysics.

In the light of this major difference, Aquinas' view of the four causes is substantially different from Aristotle's. The latter had developed his doctrine out of an analysis of change and viewed it as, basically, a production or actualization of

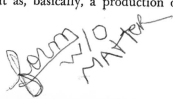

FORM W/O MATTER

forms, substantial or accidental. Aquinas, too, sees the doctrine of causes arising out of an analysis of change, but he does not view change as simply an actualization of forms. In change something is made *to be* or *to exist* in a way different from the way it existed prior to the change. Accordingly, the act of existing plays a role in change and, therefore, effects a different outlook on the four causes.

Further elucidation of this Thomistic doctrine will be left to the text and footnotes. The translation is taken from the Latin text edited by John J. Pauson.

The Principles of Nature

Chapter I

Being in Potency and Being in Act

(1) There are certain things which can exist but do not, and others which do exist. Those which can be are said to exist *in potency*, whereas those which are, are said to exist *in act*.[1] Now there are two ways of existing in act: to exist *essentially* or *substantially* (as when a man exists), and to exist *accidentally* (as when a man exists as white). The former is to exist without qualification, whereas the latter is to exist in a qualified way.[2]

(2) Something is in potency to both the ways of existing in act. Sperm and menstrual blood, for example, are in potency to being man, whereas a man is in potency to being white. Both that which is in potency to exist substantially, and that which is in potency to exist accidently, can, like the sperm and the man, respectively, be called matter. They differ, however, in this: the matter that is in potency to exist substantially is called *matter from which*,[3] whereas the matter that is in potency to exist accidentally is called *matter in*

---

[1] Aristotle, *Metaphysics* IX. 3. 1047a–b2; 6, 1048a27–b6. Cf. St. Thomas, *In IX Meta.*, lect. 3, nos. 1804–1805; lect. 5, nos. 1824–1825; *In V Meta.*, lect. 9, no. 897; *Summa Theologiae*, I, 77, 1c; *On Being and Essence*, chap. IV (p. 51 below); *De Spiritualibus Creaturis*, 1c.

[2] Aristotle, *Metaphysics* V. 7, 1017a7–31; IV. 2, 1003a33–b19. Cf. St. Thomas, *In V Meta.*, lect. 9, nos. 885–894; *In IV Meta.*, lect. 1, no. 534; *On Being and Essence*, chap. VI (p. 62 below).

[3] On the question of form making matter be, cf. a few lines below; also par. 17. See St. Thomas, *Summa Contra Gentiles*, II, 43 and 54; *Summa Theologiae*, I, 78, 1 ad 5; I, 77, 7c; *In I Phy.*, lect. 13, no. 111; *In V Meta.*, lect. 2, no. 775; *On Being and Essence*, chaps. II and VI (pp. 36 and 62 below). Cf. Aristotle, *Metaphysics* VI. 1, 1028a10–20.

which. Likewise, properly speaking, what is in potency to exist substantially is called *prime matter,* whereas what is in potency to exist accidentally is called a *subject*. Accordingly, accidents are said to be in a subject, but substantial form is not spoken of in this way. Wherefore matter differs from subject, inasmuch as a subject does not have an act of existing from that which accrues to it, but is complete with an act of existing in itself; for example, a man does not have an act of existing from whiteness. But matter has an act of existing from what accrues to it, because of itself it exists incompletely. Hence, simply put, form makes matter exist, whereas an accident does not make a subject exist. The subject, however, makes an accident exist.[4] Occasionally, however, one term is substituted for the other—that is, matter for subject, and vice versa.

(3) Moreover, just as everything in potency can be called matter, so anything from which something exists, either substantially or accidentally, can be called a form,[5] as man, since he is potentially white, becomes actually white through whiteness, and the sperm, since it is potentially man, becomes actually man through the soul.[6] Because form makes something exist actually, it is said to be an act. What makes something exist substantially is called *substantial form,* and what makes something exist accidentally is called *accidental form*.

(4) As generation is a movement to form, there are two kinds of generation corresponding to the two kinds of form: *generation simply* corresponds to substantial form, and *qualified generation* corresponds to accidental form.[7] For

---

[4] On accidents and the act of existing, see *Summa Theologiae,* I, 28, 2c; *On Being and Essence,* chap. VI (p. 62 below).

[5] See St. Thomas, *In VII Meta.,* lect. 2, no. 1278; *On Being and Essence,* chaps. II and IV (pp. 36 and 51 below); *Summa Theologiae,* I, 66, 1c and 2c; 76, 4c; 77, 6c.

[6] Aristotle, *On the Soul* II. I, 412a20–413a10. Cf. St. Thomas, *Summa Theologiae,* I, 76, 1c; *Summa Contra Gentiles,* II, 68; *On the Soul,* 1c; *De Spiritualibus Creaturis,* 2c.

[7] Aristotle, *Physics* V. 1, 224b35–225a20; *On Generation and Corruption* I. 5, 320a26–27. Cf. St. Thomas, *In V Phy.,* lect. 2, nos. 650–655; *On Being and Essence,* chap. II (p. 36).

when a substantial form is introduced, something is said to have come into being without qualification, as we have said. For example, a man comes into being, or a man is generated. When, however, an accidental form is introduced, something is said not to have come into being, but to have become this. For example, when a man becomes white, we do not say that the man comes into being or is generated without qualification, but rather that the man becomes, or is made, white.

(5) There are two kinds of corruption opposed to these two kinds of generation: *corruption simply* and *qualified corruption*. Generation simply and corruption simply occur only in the genus *substance,* whereas qualified generation and qualified corruption occur in all other genera.[8] Furthermore, as generation is a kind of passage from not-existing to existing, and, conversely, corruption a passage from existing to not-existing, generation does not arise from any nonentity but from a nonentity which is a being in potency.[9] For example, a statue comes from bronze, which is a statue in potency, not in act.

(6) Therefore, three things are required for generation: namely, a being in potency, which is matter; a state of not-existing in act, which is privation; [10] and that through which something comes to be actually, which is form.[11] Thus when a statue is made from bronze, the bronze, which is in potency to the form *statue,* is the matter. The lack of configuration or arrangement is the privation.

(7) The shape from which it gets the name *statue* is the form. This is, however, not a substantial form because the bronze, before the advent of that form, had an act of existing, and its act of existing does not depend upon that shape.[12]

8 Aristotle, *Physics* I. 7, 190a32–36; *On Generation and Corruption* I. 4, 319b9–24; I. 5, 320a10–34. Cf. St. Thomas, *In I Phy.,* lect. 12, no. 107.

9 Aristotle, *Physics* V. 1, 224b35–225a29. Cf. St. Thomas, *In V Phy.,* lect. 2, nos. 650–655; *De Veritate,* q. 5, a. 2 ad 6; *Summa Theologiae,* I, 27, 2c.

10 Aristotle, *Metaphysics* X. 4, 1055b3–29. Cf. St. Thomas, *In X Meta.,* lect. 6, nos. 2043–2048; *De Potentia,* q. 9, a. 7 ad 11.

11 Aristotle, *Metaphysics* VIII. 5, 1044b21–29. Cf. St. Thomas, *In VIII Meta.,* lect. 4, no. 1746; *Summa Theologiae* I, 66, 1 c and 2 c.

12 See above, note 6.

It is an accidental form, as are all artificial forms; [13] for art works only on what is already constituted as existing by nature.

Chapter II

Matter, Form, and Privation

(8) Therefore, there are three principles of nature: matter, form, and privation. One of these, form, is that toward which generation moves, whereas the other two lie on the side of that from which generation proceeds. Hence, matter and privation refer to the same subject, but according to different aspects. For the very same thing is both bronze and deprived-of-a-certain-shape before the advent of the form. But it is said to be bronze for one reason, and deprived-of-a-shape for another. Wherefore privation is said to be, not an essential principle, but an accidental one, since it coincides with matter.[14] Thus we say that a physician builds accidentally, for he does not build by virtue of being a physician but because he is a builder; this characteristic resides in the same subject along with his medical skill.

(9) Now accidents are of two kinds: *necessary,* which are not separated from a certain kind of thing,[15] like risibility from man, and *non-necessary,*[16] which are so separated, as is whiteness from man. Accordingly, although privation is an accidental principle, it does not follow that it is unnecessary for generation. For matter is never lacking privation: inasmuch as it is under one form, it is deprived of another, and

13 St. Thomas, *Summa Theologiae,* III, 66, 4c; *In V Meta.,* lect. 5, no. 818; *In VII Meta.,* lect. 2, no. 1277; *In VIII Meta.,* lect. 3, no. 1719.

14 Aristotle, *Physics* II. 3, 195a33–195b3. Cf. St. Thomas, *In II Phy.,* lect. 6, no. 190.

15 Aristotle, *Metaphysics* V. 30, 1025a30–35. Cf. St. Thomas, *In V Meta.,* lect. 22, nos. 1142–1143; *Summa Theologiae,* I-II, 2, 6c; I, 77, 6 ad 3; *De Spiritualibus Creaturis,* 11c; *On Being and Essence,* chap. VI (p. 62 below).

16 Aristotle, *Metaphysics* V. 30, 1025a13–19. Cf. St. Thomas, *In V Meta.,* lect. 22, nos. 1139–1141.

vice versa. For example, in fire there is the privation of air; in air there is the privation of fire.[17]

(10) Although generation is from not-existing, one should realize that we maintain, not that negation is a principle, but rather that privation is, for negation does not determine a subject for itself.[18] Lack of sight can be attributed even to nonentities, for example, "Chimeras do not see." Likewise, we can attribute it to beings that are not meant to see, such as a stone. But privation is attributed only to a determinate subject in which the missing perfection is meant to be. For example, blindness is attributed only to those things that were born to see.[19]

(11) Moreover, it is in accordance with the fact that generation does not arise from non-being simply,[20] but from non-being which is in some subject—and not just any subject, but a determined one—that privation is said to be a principle. For not everything which is not-burning will burn, but only

[17] Aquinas is using here a very ancient theory of "chemical elements." He elaborates upon his notion of element below, pars. 21 and 22. The theory has a long history, dating back at least to the pre-Socratic philosopher Empedocles (*ca.* 495–435 B.C.), who had claimed that the things of experience are composed in various ways of four opposed and irreducible elements: fire, water, earth, and air. Many subsequent Greek thinkers, including Aristotle, maintained this division, and Aquinas continues in this tradition. Modern chemistry continues this tradition in a modified way, at least in the sense that it, too, sees all physical realities to be made up of, and reducible to, approximately one hundred elements, which are chemically irreducible to one another. See *McGraw-Hill Encyclopedia of Science and Technology* (New York: McGraw-Hill, Inc., 1960), I, 652; IV, 544. For Empedocles, see Milton C. Nahm, *Selections From Early Greek Philosophy,* 3rd edn. (New York: Appleton-Century-Crofts, 1947), pp. 131 ff. For Aristotle, see *Metaphysics* V. 3, 1014a26 ff.; *On Generation and Corruption* II. 3, 330a30–331a6. For St. Thomas, cf. *In V Meta.,* lect. 4, no. 800; *Summa Theologiae,* I, 85, 8 ad 1; I, 66, 1c.

[18] Aristotle, *Metaphysics* IV. 2, 1004a9–19. Cf. St. Thomas, *In IV Meta.,* lect. 3, nos. 564–566.

[19] On negations and privations, see Aristotle, *Metaphysics* IV. 2, 1004a16. Cf. St. Thomas, *In IV Meta.,* lect. 3, no. 565; *Summa Theologiae,* I, 17, 4c; I–II, 46, 1c; *Summa Contra Gentiles,* I, 71; III, 7; *De Malo,* q. 2, a. 12 ad 3.

[20] Aristotle, *Physics* I. 7, 190a12–16. Cf. St. Thomas, *In I Phy.,* lect. 12, no. 104.

those things that are apt to burn. Privation differs, however, from the other principles, which are principles both in being and in becoming. For something to become a statue, bronze and finally the figure of a statue are necessary. Moreover, when the statue does actually exist, both of these exist. Privation, however, is a principle in becoming but not in being, because while the statue is coming into being the statue cannot exist. For if it did already exist, the statue could not come into being, since what comes to be exists only successively, as do time and change.[21] But when the statue exists, no privation of *statue* is present in it. Just as affirmation and negation cannot exist simultaneously, so neither can privation and the form of which it is the privation. Accordingly, privation is an accidental principle, as has previously been explained; the other two are essential principles.

(12) From what has been said it is evident that matter differs by definition from form and privation. For matter is that in which both form and privation are understood, as one shape and the lack of another shape are understood in bronze. Indeed, sometimes matter is given a name which includes a privation and sometimes not. So bronze, when it is the matter of a statue, does not connote a privation, because in saying "bronze" we do not include in our comprehension the lack of an arrangement or shape. But flour, since it is matter with respect to bread, includes the privation of the form of bread, because in saying "flour," one signifies that lack of disposition or ordination which is opposed to the form of bread. And so, because in generation the matter or subject remains but the privation and the composite of matter and privation do not, therefore matter that does not include privation is permanent, whereas matter that does is transient.

(13) We should realize, however, that some matter includes a form, like the bronze which is the matter of a statue. Bronze itself is a composite of matter and form. Accordingly,

21 Aristotle, *Physics* IV. 10, 217b29–220a26. Cf. St. Thomas, *In IV Phy.,* lect. 15, nos. 558 and 589; *Summa Theologiae,* I, 53, 3c; I–II, 113, 7 ad 5; *Summa Contra Gentiles,* I, 66.

since it possesses matter, bronze cannot be called prime matter. Only that matter which is understood [22] without any form or privation, but which is subject to form and privation, is called prime matter, inasmuch as there is no other matter prior to it. It is also called "hyle." [23]

(14) Since all cognition and every definition are through form,[24] it follows that prime matter can be known or defined, not of itself, but through the composite. Accordingly, we know prime matter as that which is related to all forms and privations, as bronze is related to the form of a statue and to the privation of some shape. It is called *primary* without qualification. Something can be called "prime matter" with respect to a certain genus, as water is prime matter to the genus of liquids.[25] But this is not primary without qualification, because it is a composite of matter and form; hence there is a matter prior to it.

(15) We should note that prime matter, and even form, are neither generated nor corrupted, inasmuch as every generation is from something to something.[26] That from which generation arises is matter; that to which it proceeds is form. If, therefore, matter and form were generated, there would have to be a matter of matter and a form of form *ad infinitum.* Hence, properly speaking, only composites are generated.

(16) We should note also that prime matter is said to be numerically one in all things. Something can be said to be

22 The clause "which is understood" is important, since it emphasizes St. Thomas' belief that prime matter never exists in isolation from substantial form, but can be understood as distinct from it. See below, par. 17. Cf. St. Thomas, *De Potentia*, q. 4, a. 1c.

23 In his *On Generation and Corruption* (338b26–329b2), Aristotle gives some history of this notion along with his own views. Cf. St. Thomas, *On Being and Essence*, chap. II (p. 43); *Summa Theologiae*, I, 4, 1c. The term "hyle" is a transliteration of the Greek word ὕλη, meaning "matter" or "material."

24 Aristotle, *Metaphysics* VII. 6, 1031b7. Cf. St. Thomas. *In VII Meta.*, lect. 5, no. 1365; *In V Meta.*, lect. 2, no. 764; *Summa Theologiae*, I, 34, I ad 3; *De Veritate*, q. 1, a. 1c; q. 7, a. 8c.

25 See above, note 17.

26 Aristotle, *Metaphysics* XII. 3, 1069b35–1070a1. Cf. St. Thomas, *In XII Meta.*, lect. 3, nos. 2442–2443.

numerically one in two ways. First, it can be numerically one if it has one numerically determinate form, like Socrates. Prime matter is not said to be numerically one in this way, since in itself it does not have any form. Something can be numerically one in another way, that is, if it lacks the dispositions through which numerical differences occur. Prime matter is said to be numerically one in this way, since it is understood without dispositions by which numerical differences occur.

(17) Finally we note that although prime matter does not in itself have any form or privation, as in the nature of bronze there is neither shape nor the lack of shape, nevertheless prime matter never exists without form and privation. Sometimes it is under one form, sometimes it is under another. But matter cannot exist of itself, since of itself it possesses no form. It does not exist in act, since existing in act occurs only through a form,[27] but exists only in potency. Hence whatever exists in act cannot be called prime matter.

Chapter III

Causes, Principles, and Elements

(18) From what has been said, it is evident that there are three principles of nature: matter, form, and privation. These alone, however, are not sufficient for generation. For what is in potency cannot reduce itself to act.[28] Bronze, which is in potency to being a statue, does not make itself be a statue, but needs an agent which draws out the form of statue from potency to act. For form cannot draw itself out from potency to act. Here I am speaking of the form of the thing generated, which we have already said is the term of generation. This form exists only when a change is completed, but the agent

[27] See above, note 5.
[28] Aristotle, *Physics* VII. 1, 241b24–243a4. Cf. St. Thomas, *In VII Phy.*, lects. 1 and 2, nos. 885–896.

itself exists only during the becoming—that is, while the thing is coming to be.[29] There is required, therefore, besides form and matter, another principle which acts. This is called the *efficient* or *moving cause,* or agent, or that from which the motion begins.

(19) Because, as Aristotle states in Book Two of the *Metaphysics,* [30] everything that acts, acts only when intending something, a fourth principle is required—that is, what is intended by the agent. This is called the *end.* And although every agent, be it natural or voluntary, intends an end, we should realize nevertheless that it does not follow that every agent knows or deliberates about the end. Knowing the end is necessary for those whose actions are not determined, but for whom opposed goals are possible, as is the case for voluntary agents. These, therefore, must know the end, through which knowledge they determine their actions. However, the actions of natural agents are determined; hence, there is no necessity for their choosing the means to their end. Avicenna offers the example of the cithara [31] player, who need not deliberate as to which notes form a chord by striking each individually, since they are predetermined. If the player did deliberate, there would be a delay between the notes, producing an arpeggio. Furthermore, deliberation is especially apparent in the voluntary agent, as opposed to the natural agent. So an even stronger argument can be made if one sees that if a voluntary agent (whose deliberation is especially evident) does not always deliberate, then, certainly, neither does the natural agent. Therefore, it is possible for a natural agent to intend an end without deliberating about it.[32] To

[29] Aristotle, *Physics* II. 3, 195b17–21. Cf. St. Thomas, *In II Phy.,* lect. 4, nos. 194–195; *Summa Contra Gentiles,* I, 13; cf. below, par. 34.

[30] Aristotle, *Metaphysics* II. 2, 994b8–16. Cf. St. Thomas, *In II Meta.,* lect. 4, nos. 316–319. Aristotle, *Metaphysics* V. 2, 1013a33–34. Cf. St. Thomas, *In V Meta.,* lect. 2, nos. 771, 775.

[31] An ancient musical instrument resembling a lyre, and a precursor of the zither.

[32] On the relations between ends and Creator, see *Summa Theologiae,* I, 19, 4c; *Summa Contra Gentiles,* II, 2, 23; *De Potentia,* q. 1, a. 5.

intend in this way is nothing more than to have a natural inclination toward something.

(20) From what has been said it is evident that there are four causes, namely, material, efficient, formal, and final. Moreover, although "principle" and "cause" are said quasi-interchangeably, as is maintained in Book Five of the *Metaphysics*,[33] nevertheless, Aristotle in his *Physics*[34] contends that there are four causes and three principles. Furthermore, he holds that causes are both extrinsic and intrinsic. Matter and form are said to be intrinsic to a thing inasmuch as they are constitutive parts of a thing, whereas the efficient and the final causes are called extrinsic, since they are external to the thing. But he accepts only intrinsic causes as principles. Privation is not included among the causes, for, as has been said, it is an accidental principle. When we speak of four causes, therefore, we mean essential causes.[35] Accidental causes, however, are reduced to essential ones, since everything that is accidental is reduced to that which is essential.[36]

(21) But although Aristotle contends in Book One of the *Physics* [37] that principles are intrinsic causes, nevertheless, as he states in Book Eleven of the *Metaphysics*,[38] principle is properly said to be an extrinsic cause, whereas those causes which are parts of a thing—that is, the intrinsic causes— are called *elements*.[39] However, both can be said to be causes,

[33] Aristotle, *Metaphysics* V. 1, 1013a14–21. Cf. St. Thomas, *In V Meta.*, lect. 1, nos. 751–760.

[34] Aristotle, *Physics* I. 7, 191a14–23. Cf. St. Thomas, *In I Phy.*, lect. 13, nos. 118–119. Aristotle, *Physics* II. 3, 105a15–16. Cf. St. Thomas, *In II Phy.*, lect. 5, nos. 183–186. Aristotle, *Physics* II. 7, 198a14–24. Cf. St. Thomas, *In II Phy.*, lect. 10, nos. 239–240.

[35] See above, note 16.

[36] St. Thomas, *Summa Theologiae*, I, 28, 2c; *Quodlibet*, IX, 3 ad 2.

[37] Aristotle, *Physics* I. 7, 190b17–191a23. Cf. St. Thomas, *In I Phy.*, lect. 13, nos. 110–119.

[38] Aristotle, *Metaphysics* XII. 4, 1070b22–30. Cf. St. Thomas, *In XII Meta.*, lect. 4, nos. 2464–2472. (Because of the discrepancy between ancient and modern Aristotelian texts, Aquinas' book references frequently do not coincide with contemporary book divisions.)

[39] See above, note 17. Further explanation is made below, par. 22.

although sometimes one is taken for the other. For every cause can be said to be a principle, and every principle a cause. But cause appears to connote something more than what is commonly said to be a principle, inasmuch as anything that is prior, whether or not something else follows from it, can be said to be a principle. An artisan is called the principle of a knife, for example, because a knife comes into being as a result of his activity. But when something is changed from black to white, black is said to be the principle of that motion, just as, universally, anything from which change commences is called a principle. Black, however, is not that from which the being of white follows. Something prior is said to be a cause only when the existence of what is posterior follows from it. Hence, a cause is said to be that from whose existing another follows. Accordingly, what is prior by way of being that from which motion starts cannot be called an essential cause, even if it is called a principle. This is the reason for including privation among principles, but not among causes. A privation is that from which generation begins. It can, however, be called an accidental cause, inasmuch as it coincides with matter, as was explained above.

(22) *Element* is predicated properly only of those causes which enter into the composition of a thing, and which are properly material; every material cause, moreover, is not properly said to be an element but only that one which is involved in a thing's primary composition. Thus we do not speak of limbs as elements of man, because his limbs are composed of other things. We do claim, however, that earth and water are elements; for these are not composed of other bodies, rather it is from these that the first composition of natural bodies results. Hence Aristotle, in Book Five of his *Metaphysics*,[40] says that an element is "an immanent, specifically irreducible entity of which a thing is primarily composed." The explanation of the phrase, "of which a thing is primarily composed" is clear from what we have already said. The word "imma-

40 Aristotle, *Metaphysics* V. 2, 1014a26–28. Cf. St. Thomas, *In V Meta.*, lect. 4, nos. 795–798.

nent" is used to differentiate an element from that other kind of matter which is totally destroyed by generation, like the bread which is the matter of blood. Blood is generated only if bread is destroyed. Bread does not remain in blood, and therefore it cannot be said to be an element of blood. But elements must remain in some way, since they are not entirely destroyed, as is stated in the book *On Generation*.[41] The phrase "specifically irreducible" differentiates the elements from those materials having parts diverse in form— that is, in species—like a hand, whose parts are flesh and bone, which are specifically different. But an element is not divided into specifically diverse parts; any part of the element water, for example, is water. Nor is it necessary for an element to be undivided quantitatively in order to be an element. It suffices that it not be divided specifically. If it is not divided in any way, it is also called an element, as letters are said to be elements of words. From all that we have said it is clear, therefore, that a principle is in some way more than a cause, and a cause more than an element. This is, indeed, what the Commentator contends in his comment on the fifth book of the *Metaphysics*.[42]

Chapter IV

The Relationships Between Causes

(23) Having seen that there are four kinds of cause, it is also necessary to see that it is not impossible for the same thing to have several causes, like a statue, which has both bronze and an artisan as causes. The artisan is the efficient

[41] Aristotle, *On Generation and Corruption* I. 10, 327b22–31. For a modern discussion of this point, see Pierre Hoenen, S. J., *Cosmologia*, 3rd edn. (Rome: Gregorian U. Press, 1945), pp. 280–300.

[42] The "Commentator" in medieval scholastic literature was almost always Averroes (ibn-Rushd), 1126–1198, a Spanish Moslem lawyer, physician, and philosopher, who was a staunch follower of, and commentator upon, the works of Aristotle. Aquinas refers here to his *Aristotelis Metaphysicorum libri XIIII cum Averrois Cordubensis in eosdem Commentariis et Epitome* (Venice: apud Iuntas, 1574), Bk. V. chap. 3, t. 4.

cause, and the bronze the material one. Nor is it impossible for the same thing to be the cause of contraries, as the pilot is the cause of both the safety and the sinking of his ship. He is the cause of the latter by his absence, and of the former by his presence.

(24) It should be understood also that it is possible for the same thing to be a cause and to be caused, with respect to the same thing but in different ways. For example, taking a walk is the efficient cause of health, while health is the final cause of taking a walk, inasmuch as taking a walk is sometimes done for the sake of health. Likewise, the body is the matter of the soul, and the soul is the form of the body. The efficient cause is said to be a cause with respect to the end, since the end does not exist in act unless the agent acts; but the end is said to be the cause of the efficient cause, since the latter does not operate except through the intention of an end. Hence, an efficient cause is the cause of that which is the end, as in the example of taking a walk for one's health. It does not, however, make the end be an end, and therefore it is not the cause of the causality of the end—that is, it does not make the end be a final cause. A physician, for example, produces actual health, but he does not establish health as an end. Moreover, the end does not cause that which is the efficient cause, rather, it is a cause of the efficient cause's being an efficient cause. For health—and I mean the health resulting from the physician's ministrations—does not make a physician be a physician; it causes him to be an efficient cause. Hence, the end is the cause of the causality of the efficient cause, for it makes the efficient cause be an efficient cause. Similarly, it makes the matter be matter, and form be form, since matter receives a form only for some end, and a form perfects matter only for an end. Wherefore the end is said to be the cause of causes, inasmuch as it is the cause of the causality of all the causes. Matter is also said to be the cause of a form, inasmuch as a form does not exist except in matter. Similarly, form is the cause of matter, inasmuch as matter does not actually exist except through form. Matter and form are mutually related,

as the second book of the *Physics* states.[43] They are related to
the composite, as parts are to the whole and as the simple is
to the complex.

(25) Every cause, insofar as it is a cause, is naturally prior
to what is caused.[44] We should realize, however, that priority
can have two forms, as Aristotle says in Book Sixteen of
On Animals.[45] Accordingly, a thing can be called prior and
posterior, and a cause can be called caused, with respect to
the same thing. For one thing can be called prior to another
in generation and time, or in substance and completeness.
Therefore, since the operation of nature proceeds from the
imperfect to the perfect and from the incomplete to the complete, the imperfect is prior to the perfect in generation and
time, but the perfect is prior to the imperfect in substance.
For example, a man can be said to be prior to a boy in substance and completeness, whereas a boy is prior to a man
in generation and time. But, although in things generable
the imperfect is prior to the perfect, and potency prior to act
—considering, in one and the same thing, that what is prior
is imperfect rather than perfect, and in potency rather than
in act—nevertheless, speaking without qualification, what is
in act and perfect must be prior. This follows because what
reduces a potency to act is in act, and what perfects the imperfect is itself perfect.[46] Matter, indeed, is prior to form in
generation and time,[47] inasmuch as that to which something is
added is prior to that which is added. But form is prior to

[43] Aristotle, *Physics* II. 2, 194b9–10. Cf. St. Thomas, *In II Phy.*, lect. 4,
no. 174.

[44] On kinds of priority, see Aristotle, *Metaphysics* V. 11, 1018b9–1019a14.
Cf. St. Thomas, *In V Meta.*, lect. 13, nos. 936–953.

[45] Aristotle, *On the Generation of Animals* II. 6, 742a21.

[46] Aristotle, *Metaphysics* IX. 8, 1049b23–28. Cf. St. Thomas, *In IX Meta.*,
lect. 7, nos. 1848–1849. Aristotle, *Metaphysics* IX. 9, 1051a4. Cf. St.
Thomas, *In IX Meta.*, lect. 11, no. 1882; *Summa Contra Gentiles*, I, 28.

[47] Aristotle, *Metaphysics* IX. 8, 1049b18–26. Cf. St. Thomas, *In IX
Meta.*, lect. 7, nos. 1847–1848; *In VII Meta.*, lect. 2, 1278. Aristotle, *Metaphysics* XII. 6, 1071b22–26. Cf. St. Thomas, *In XII Meta.*, lect. 5, no.
2494; *In XII Meta.*, lect. 6, no. 2506.

matter in substance and in fully constituted being,[48] because matter has complete existence only through form. Similarly, the efficient cause is prior to the end in generation and time,[49] since the motion to the end comes about by the efficient cause; but the end is prior to the efficient cause [50] as such in substance and completeness, since the action of the efficient cause is completed only through the end. Therefore, the material and the efficient causes are prior by way of generation, whereas form and end are prior by way of perfection.

(26) It should be noted that necessity is of two kinds: *absolute* and *conditional*.[51] Necessity is indeed absolute when it proceeds from causes which are prior by way of generation, that is, from the material and efficient causes. For example, the necessity of death stems from matter—that is, from the disposition of composing contraries; therefore it is said to be absolute because there is no impediment to it. This is also called the necessity of matter. However, conditional necessity proceeds from causes posterior in generation, that is, from form and end. Accordingly, we say that conception must take place if a man is to be generated. This necessity is said to be conditional, because it is not necessary without qualification for some particular woman to conceive. However, conception

[48] Aristotle, *Metaphysics* IX. 8, 1049b3–1051a3. Cf. St. Thomas, *In IX Meta.*, lect. 7, 8, 9, nos. 1844–1882.

[49] Aristotle, *Metaphysics* V. 11, 1019a5–10. Cf. St. Thomas, *In V Meta.*, lect. 13, nos. 950–952.

[50] Aristotle, *Physics* II. 3, 195a8–11. Cf. St. Thomas, *In II Phy.*, lect. 5, no. 182. Aristotle, *Metaphysics* II. 2, 994b9–10. Cf. St. Thomas, *In III Meta.*, lect. 4, no. 378; *In V Meta.*, lect. 2, no. 775; *In I Meta.*, lect. 4, no. 70; *In II Meta.*, lect. 4, No. 316.

[51] Aristotle, *Metaphysics* V. 5, 1015a20–b15. Cf. St. Thomas, *In V Meta.*, lect. 6, nos. 827–841; *Summa Theologiae*, I, 41, 2 ad 5; I, 82, 1c; *De Veritate*, q. 17, a. 3c. Aquinas is echoing here an early medieval author, Boethius (*ca.* 475–525), who was very influential on later medieval thinkers. On these two kinds of necessity, see his *Consolation of Philosophy*, trans. Richard Green, "The Library of Liberal Arts," No. 86 (New York: The Liberal Arts Press, Inc., 1962), pp. 117–118.

is necessary under this condition, namely, if a man is to be generated. This is called the necessity of the end.[52]

(27) We should also realize that three of the causes—form, end, and efficient cause [53]—can coincide. The generation of fire offers a clear example of this. Fire generates fire; therefore fire is an efficient cause, insofar as it generates. Fire is a form, insofar as it makes that which formerly was in potency be in act. Finally, fire is an end, insofar as it is intended by the agent and insofar as the operation of the agent is terminated in it. There are, however, two kinds of ends, namely, the end of the generation process and the end of the thing generated.[54] Both of these ends are evident in producing a knife. The form *knife* is the end of the generating process; but cutting, which is the knife's operation, is the end of the thing generated—that is, the knife.

(28) Sometimes the end of the generating process coincides with the two other above-mentioned causes: form and efficient cause. This occurs when generation proceeds from one thing to another thing that is similar in species to the first, as when a man generates a man, or an olive tree an olive tree. It is not possible, however, for the end of the thing generated to coincide with the form and the efficient cause; yet we should realize that the end and the form are numerically identical, inasmuch as the form of the thing generated and the end of the generation are numerically the same.[55] The end of the generating process and the efficient cause coincide in species, but not in number.[56] For it is impossible for the maker and the thing made to be the same in number; but they can be

[52] Aristotle, *On Generation and Corruption* II. 11, 337b10–338a17. Cf. St. Thomas *Summa Theologiae,* I, 82, 1c; *Summa Contra Gentiles,* II, 30.

[53] Aristotle, *Physics* II. 7, 198a25–27. Cf. St. Thomas, *In II Phy.*, lect. 11, no. 242; *In VII Meta.*, lect. 6, no. 1392; *In VIII Meta.*, lect. 4, no. 1737.

[54] Aristotle, *Physics* II. 2, 194a35. Cf. St. Thomas, *In II Phy.*, lect. 4, nos. 172–173; *In I Meta.*, lect. 4, no. 71; *Summa Theologiae,* I–II, 1, 8c.

[55] Aristotle, *Physics* II. 7, 198a25–28. Cf. St. Thomas, *In II Phy.*, lect. 11, no. 242; *In VII Meta.*, lect. 6, no. 1392; *In VIII Meta.*, lect. 4, no. 1737.

[56] Aristotle, *Physics* II. 7, 198a25–28. Cf. St. Thomas, *In II Phy.*, lect. 11, no. 242; *In VII Meta.*, lect. 6, no. 1392.

the same in species. For example, when a man generates a man, the man generating and the man generated are diverse in number, but the same in species.

(29) Matter does not coincide with any of the other causes, since, by reason of the fact that it is being in potency, matter is by nature imperfect.[57] The other causes, however, since they are in act, have the nature of something perfect. The perfect and the imperfect do not coincide.

Chapter V

Other Divisions of the Causes

(30) Wherefore, having seen that there are four causes, namely, efficient, material, formal, and final, we should also realize that each of these causes can be divided in many ways. There exist what are called *prior* and *posterior* causes.[58] For example, both the physician's art and the physician himself are causes of health, but the art is a prior cause and the physician a posterior one. The same division is true of the formal cause and the other causes. Note also that we should always reduce a question to the first cause.[59] If we were to ask, "Why is the man healthy?" we would answer, "Because the physician healed him." Continuing, we would ask, "But by what means did the physician heal?"—"Through the art of healing that he possesses."

(31) Moreover, we must understand that *proximate cause* [60] means the same as *posterior cause*, and *remote cause* the same as *prior cause*. Accordingly, these two divisions of causes—prior and posterior, and remote and proximate—signify the

---

57 Aristotle, *Metaphysics* VIII. 2, 1042b9–1043a28. Cf. St. Thomas, *In VIII Meta.*, lect. 2, nos. 1691–1701; *In V Meta.*, lect. 3, no. 779; *In II Phy.*, lect. 11, no. 247.

58 St. Thomas, *In V Meta.*, lect. 3, no. 785.

59 St. Thomas, *In V Meta.*, lect. 3, no. 758; *Summa Contra Gentiles*, II, 21 and 42.

60 Aristotle, *Metaphysics* V. 2, 1013b28–34. Cf. St. Thomas, *In V Meta.*, lect. 3, no. 785; *In VI Meta.*, lect. 3, no. 1198; *Summa Theologiae*, I, 14, 13 ad 1.

same thing. Furthermore, we should observe that the more universal cause is always called the remote cause, while the more particular cause is called the proximate cause. For example, the proximate form of man is his definition, that is, *rational mortal animal;* but animal is more remote, and substance even further removed. For all superior things are forms of inferior ones. Similarly, the proximate matter of a statue is bronze, while the remote matter is metal, and the more remote is body.

(32) There is likewise another division of causes: into *essential* and *accidental* causes.[61] A cause is called essential when it causes something by reason of its being what it is, as, for example, the builder is the cause of a house,[62] and the wood is the matter of a bench. A cause is called accidental when it happens to coincide with an essential cause. This may be illustrated by a grammarian who builds something. The grammarian is said to be an accidental cause of a building, not insofar as he is a grammarian, but insofar as being a grammarian is accidental to building. The same is true of the other causes.

(33) In addition, certain causes are *simple,* and others *composite.*[63] A cause is called simple when it alone is said to be the cause, be it essential (as when we say that the builder is the cause of the house) or accidental (as when we say that the physician is the cause of the house). However, we would be speaking of a composite cause when both are called the cause, as when we say that the builder-physician is the cause of the house. A simple cause can also be defined, according

[61] Aristotle, *Metaphysics* V. 2, 1013b34–1014a26. Cf. St. Thomas, *In V Meta.,* lect. 3, nos. 783–784; Aristotle, *Physics* II. 3, 195a28–b3. Cf. St. Thomas, *In II Phy.,* lect. 6, nos. 187–190; *De Potentia,* q. 3, a. 6, ad 6.

[62] The builder is similar to what he causes in his knowledge of what he causes. Cf. *De Potentia,* VII, 7c.

[63] Aristotle, *Metaphysics* V. 2, 1014a19. Cf. St. Thomas, *In V Meta.,* lect. 3, nos. 792–793. Aristotle, *Physics* II. 3, 195b16. Cf. St. Thomas, *In II Phy.,* lect. 6, no. 193.

to Avicenna,[64] as that which causes without being united with another, like bronze which causes the statue without the addition of any other matter. Further illustrations might be the physician who produces health, or the fire that warms. A cause is called composite when many things must unite into being a cause, as not one man, but many, are the cause of the motion of a ship, and not one stone, but many are the matter of the house.

(34) In addition, certain causes are *actual*, and others *potential*.[65] A cause is actual when it is actually causing the thing, like a builder when he builds, or the bronze from which a statue is being made. A potential cause is one which, although not actually causing the thing, nevertheless can cause something, like a builder when he is not building. It should be understood in speaking of actual causes that what causes and what is caused must exist simultaneously, such that if the one exists, the other does also. For if there is an actual builder, he must be building, and if actual building is going on, the builder must be a builder in act. This is not necessary, however, in those causes which are causes only in potency.

(35) Moreover, we should realize that a universal cause is related to a universal effect, while a singular cause is related to a singular effect.[66] For example, the builder is the cause of the house, while *this* builder is the cause of *this* house.

---

[64] Avicenna (ibn-Sina), 980–1037, a Moslem philosopher and physician, highly regarded by the 13th-century Scholastics. He was an Aristotelian with neoplatonic tendencies. Aquinas' reference is to his *Sufficentiae* (Venice, 1508), Bk. I, chap. 12B.

[65] Aristotle, *Physics* II. 3, 195b5. Cf. St. Thomas, *In II Phy.*, lect. 6, no. 191. Aristotle, *Metaphysics* V. 2, 1014a20–26. Cf. St. Thomas, *In V Meta.*, lect. 3, nos. 790–791.

[66] Aristotle, *Physics* II. 3, 195b25–28. Cf. St. Thomas, *In II Phy.*, lect. 6, no. 197. Aristotle, *Metaphysics* V. 2, 1014a10–13. Cf. St. Thomas, *In V Meta.*, lect. 3, no. 791.

Chapter VI

Unity and Diversity Within Causes

(36) It should be understood that in speaking of the intrinsic principles matter and form, there are a similarity and a difference of principles, according to the similarity and the difference of things resulting from the principles. Certain things are the same numerically, like Socrates (when Socrates is being pointed at) and this man. Others are diverse numerically but the same specifically, like Socrates and Plato, who, although they are the same in human species, nevertheless differ numerically. Further, certain things are different specifically, but the same generically, like a man and an ass, which are the same in the genus *animal*. Still others are diverse generically but the same only according to an analogy, like substance and quantity, which do not agree in any genus but are similar only analogously; for they are alike only in being. Being is not a genus, however, since it is predicated, not univocally, but analogously.[67]

(37) To grasp this one should understand that something can be predicated of many things in three ways: *univocally, equivocally,* and *analogously.* A univocal predication occurs when something is predicated according to the same name and the same nature,[68] that is, definition, as *animal* is predicated both of man and of ass. Each is called an animal and each is

[67] St. Thomas' use of analogies is quite extensive and complicated, and is extremely important in his metaphysics. He never wrote a treatise explicitly on analogy, but his views on the matter can be discovered from an analysis of the analogies he uses throughout his writings. For some modern commentaries, see George P. Klubertanz, *St. Thomas on Analogy* (Chicago: Loyola University Press, 1960); H. Lyttkens, *The Analogy Between God and the World* (Uppsala: Almquist and Wiksells, 1952); G. B. Phelan, *St. Thomas and Analogy* (Milwaukee: Marquette University Press, 1941).

[68] Cf. St. Thomas, *Summa Theologiae*, I, 79, 10 ad 3; I–II, 12, 1c; *De Veritate*, q. 13, a 3c; *Summa Contra Gentiles*, I, 55.

an animated substance capable of sensation, which is the definition of an animal. Equivocal predication occurs when something is predicated of several things according to the same name but diverse natures, like *dog*, said of a barking animal and of a stellar constellation. These agree in name only, not in definition or signification, for what is signified by a name is the definition, as is stated in the fourth book of the *Metaphysics*.[69] An analogous predication occurs when something is predicated of several things which have diverse natures, but which are related to some one thing, as *healthy* is predicated of an animal body, of urine, and of medicine, although it does not wholly signify the same thing in all. For *health*y is predicated of urine as of a sign of health; of a body, as of its subject; of medicine, as of its cause. Nevertheless, each of these is related to the one end, health.

(38) Sometimes things which are similar analogously—that is, through a proportion, a comparison, or an agreement—are such by being related to one end. The example above is an instance of this. At other times things are analogous by being related to one agent.[70] For example, *physician* is predicated of one who heals through his training; of one who heals without training, like a midwife; and even of the instruments used. But it is predicated of all of them in relation to one agency, which in this case is the healing art. At still other times many things are similar analogously by attribution to one subject, as *being*, is said of substance, quantity, quality, and the other predicaments.[71] Quantity and the others are called being, but not for the same reason that substance is. All the others are called being inasmuch as they are related to substance, which indeed is their subject. Therefore, *being* is said first of substance and only secondarily of the others. Consequently, being

[69] Aristotle, *Metaphysics* IV. 7, 1012a22–23. Cf. St. Thomas, *In IV Meta.*, lect. 16, no. 731.

[70] The analogy of attribution described here is only one of the many used by St. Thomas. For a thorough analysis of this text see Klubertanz, *St. Thomas on Analogy*, pp. 38–46.

[71] See note 67.

is not the genus of substance and quantity, because no genus is predicated of some of its species first, and of others secondarily. Being is predicated analogously; and this is what we meant when we claimed that substance and quantity differ generically but are analogously the same.

(39) Therefore, of those things which are numerically the same, both the matter and the form are numerically the same,[72] as [both matter and form] of Tullius and of Cicero. Of those which are specifically the same but numerically diverse, the matter and the form are not numerically the same, but are specifically the same, as [those] of Socrates and of Plato. Similarly, of those things which are generically the same, their principles are generically the same, like the soul and the body of an ass and of a horse, which differ specifically but are the same generically. Likewise, of those things which are similar only in an analogous way, their principles are only analogously or proportionately similar. For matter and form and privation, or even potency and act, are principles of substance and of the other genera. Nevertheless, the matter of a substance and that of quantity, and likewise the form and the privation, differ generically, but agree only according to a proportion, which consists in this: just as the matter of a substance is related to the substance in the nature of matter, so too is the matter of quantity related to quantity. Accordingly, just as substance is the cause of all the other things, so the principles of substance are the principles of all the others.

---

[72] It is, of course, only a loose way of speaking to claim that there are two things which are numerically the same. Strictly, if there are two distinct individuals they are by that very fact numerically different. This is indicated by the example Aquinas uses of *Tullius* and *Cicero*, between which there is only a verbal distinction. In any one individual there is only one substantial form and matter.

On Being and Essence

Introduction to
On Being and Essence

This treatise was probably composed in the early 1250's. Aquinas was still a student at the University of Paris, where Aristotle was being read and absorbed for the first time by some of the more liberal Christian thinkers of the period. Aquinas can be considered as a member of this group. The treatise indicates, however, that while Aquinas was impressed by Aristotelian theory, he nevertheless accepted Aristotle's ideas only to the extent that they were compatible with his own metaphysical views—of which, in this treatise, we find an early explicit expression. *On Being and Essence* expounds his theory of being and its implications, the more important of which concern essence, and the reality of genera, species, and specific differences. If the problem can be put simply, Aquinas attempts here to relate his doctrine of being to certain aspects of our conceptual knowledge.

Precisely what prompted Aquinas to write this treatise is not known with certainty. We do, however, know some of the philosophical issues that plagued many of the theologians prior to and during St. Thomas' day; and it seems probable that this treatise was occasioned by these problems and by St. Thomas' desire to work through them in the light of his newly-developed metaphysics.

The introduction to *The Principles of Nature* outlines St. Thomas' metaphysics. *On Being and Essence* expands this central intuition with a consideration of the being of God, substances without matter, and material substances. In addition, Aquinas also addresses himself here, and in the light of his metaphysics, to the problem that Boethius had raised during the sixth century, when he asked what reality species, genera, and differences had. What reality, to use a concrete example, is there to rationality, animality, or rational animality? Boethius did not doubt that these things possessed a reality in the human mind. The problem was whether they had any reality apart from it. This became known as the problem of universals, and at times medieval philosophy is described exclusively in terms of this problem. Certainly it was not the only problem which the men of the Middle Ages treated, but just as surely it was one of the major ones; consequently by Aquinas' time many bitter battles had already been fought over the issue. Inasmuch as Aquinas takes up this particular problem in this treatise, he seems to want to present his own views on the problem, but only in the light of his wider metaphysical concern—that is, with the act of existing. The question for Aquinas, then, amounts to asking whether or not the various species, genera, or differences are of themselves possessed of a real act of existing, or whether their existence is purely mental.

At first sight, this treatise appears to be something like an exercise in twentieth-century linguistic analysis, that is, a problem of establishing the meaning of various terms. In reality, however, Aquinas' proposals as to the meaning of the terms "being," "essence," "species," and "genus," turns out to be a metaphysical treatise, with a strong emphasis upon the contemporary problem of the universals.

Two Latin texts of this treatise are available: the Baur text and the Roland-Gosselin text. I have chosen to use the latter as the basis for translation. Occasionally it is obvious that the Roland-Gosselin text is in error. On these occasions I have referred to the Baur text and attempted to present a more meaningful translation, and have indicated the shift in the notes. The Boyer text, mentioned occasionally in the footnotes, is an attempt to reconcile the two Latin texts.

On Being and Essence

Preface

A small error in the beginning of something is a great one at the end, as the Philosopher claims in the first book of his *On the Heavens*.[1] Moreover, being and essence are what the intellect first conceives,[2] as Avicenna maintains in the first book of his *Metaphysics*.[3] Hence we ought to state what the terms "essence" and "being" signify, how they are found in diverse things, and, finally, how they are related to logical intentions,[4] namely, genus, species, and difference. We proceed in this way in order to avoid the errors which follow from being ignorant of *being* and *essence,* and to reveal their difficulty.

Chapter I

Since a knowledge of simple things must be acquired from those that are complex, and since a knowledge of prior things must be acquired from those that are posterior—so that beginning with easier matters a discipline might more suitably proceed—we must, therefore, begin with the meaning of *being* and then take up the meaning of *essence.*

As the Philosopher states in the fifth book of the *Meta-*

[1] Aristotle, *On the Heavens* I. 5, 271b13.

[2] St. Thomas, *De Veritate,* I, 1c; *In III De An.,* lect. 8, nos. 705–719.

[3] For Avicenna, see note 64, p. 25. The reference here is to his *Metaphysica* (Venice, 1495; reprint, Louvain: Édition de la Bibliothèque S.J., 1961), tr. I, c. 6A.

[4] To know man as a species of animal is to have second intention knowledge, inasmuch as the object of that knowledge, a species, exists only (logically, that is) in the mind. See *De Potentia,* VII, 9c; *De Veritate,* q. 21, a. 3 ad 5; *Summa Theologiae,* I, q. 79, a. 10 ad 3.

physics,[5] it must be understood that *being through itself*[6] is used in two ways. In one way it is divided into the ten genera. In another way it signifies the truth of propositions. The difference between these two is that, according to the latter way, *being* can be attributed to anything concerning which an affirmative proposition can be formed, even if it posits nothing in reality. In this way even privations and negations are called beings; for we say that an affirmation *is* opposed to a negation, and that blindness *is* in the eye. But in the former way, *being* can be said only of something which exists in reality. Accordingly, in the first way, blindness and things of this kind are not beings. Therefore, the term "essence" is not derived from *being* said in the second way, for, in this way, some things are said to be beings which do not have an essence, as is evident in privations. *Essence*, however, is derived from being said in the first way. Hence the Commentator, in the same place,[7] says that *being* used in the first way signifies the essence of a thing. As we have noted, because *being* used in this way is divided into ten genera, *essence* must signify something common to all natures, through which natures diverse beings are placed in diverse genera and species. Thus, for example, humanity is the essence of man, and so with others.

Moreover, that through which something is constituted in its proper genus or species is what is signified by the definition that declares what a thing is. Hence, philosophers have substituted the name "quiddity" for that of "essence." It is what the Philosopher frequently calls "the *what* a thing was to be,"[8] that is, that through which something is a certain

---

[5] Aristotle, *Metaphysics* V. 7, 1017a22–35; cf. St. Thomas, *In V Meta.*, lect. 9, nos. 889–894.

[6] Cf. above, *The Principles of Nature*, chap. I (pp. 7–10).

[7] See note 42, p. 8. Reference here is to Averroes, *In V Meta.*, 7, t. c. 14.

[8] The Latin here is *quod quid erat esse*, which has been literally translated. It is the Latin equivalent of the famous Aristotelian expression τὸ τί ἦν εἶναι. In this section St. Thomas is calling attention to the fact

kind of being. It is called *form*,[9] moreover, inasmuch as "form" signifies the certitude of anything, as Avicenna says in the third book of his *Metaphysics*.[10] It is also called by the name "nature," when the latter is understood according to the first of those four senses which Boethius establishes in the book *De Duabus Naturis*[11]—that is, when *nature* is said of anything that can be grasped intellectually in some way. For a thing is intelligible only through its definition and essence. Accordingly, the Philosopher, in the fifth book of the *Metaphysics*,[12] states that every substance is a nature. Yet

---

that a definition is a knowledge intending that by which something is a certain kind of thing, by which it can be said to belong to a certain species. The "was" in the English equivalent does not indicate past tense; it implies, rather, the dynamism of a thing through which it perfects itself. In other words, through its form a thing is designed to be (was to be) oriented toward further fulfillment. See Aristotle, *Metaphysics* VII. 3, 1028b34; *Posterior Analytics* I. 22, 82b38. Cf. St. Thomas, *In VII Meta.*, lect. 1, nos. 1268–1269; *In I Post. Anal.*, lect. 33, nos. 6–7. On the question of perfection through action, see St. Thomas, *Summa Theologiae*, I, 60, 5c; *Summa Contra Gentiles*, III, 112.

[9] *Forma* is used here to refer, as St. Thomas indicates, to the whole essence. This, therefore, embraces in material things both the substantial form and prime matter. A discussion of *forma totius* (used here) and *forma partis* (substantial) in regard to the human soul is found in St. Thomas, *In VII Meta.*, lect. 9, no. 1467.

[10] The Roland-Gosselin text mentions here the third book of Avicenna's *Metaphysics*, whereas the Boyer text reads *in secundo Metaphysicae suae*. See Avicenna, *Metaphysica*, tr. III, c. 5A; also tr. I, c. 6C.

[11] Boethius (*ca.* 475–525), a Roman philosopher and state minister under Theodoric (454–526), king of the Ostrogoths. Boethius lost favor, was imprisoned, and while there, composed his famous *The Consolation of Philosophy*, which is still read today. The *De Persona et Duabus Naturis* to which Aquinas refers here is known today as *A Treatise Against Eutyches and Nestorius*, and is found in *The Theological Tractates and The Consolation of Philosophy* trans. by Rev. H. F. Stewart and E. K. Rand, "The Loeb Classical Library," No. 74 (Cambridge, Mass.: Harvard University Press, 1946), chap. I, pp. 77–79.

[12] Roland-Gosselin text, *in quarto Metaphysice;* Baur and Boyer both have *in quinto Metaphysicae*. In fact, Aristotle discusses nature at length in the fifth book. Reference is probably to *Metaphysics* V. 4, 1015a12. Cf. St. Thomas, *In V Meta.*, lect. 5, nos. 819 and 822.

the term *nature*, taken in this sense, seems to signify the essence of a thing inasmuch as it possesses an ordering to its proper operations, since no thing is devoid of its proper operation. The term "quiddity," however, is used to signify the definition.[13] But "essence" is used inasmuch as it designates that through which and in which a being has the act of existing.[14]

But because being is asserted absolutely and primarily of substances, and secondarily and in a relative sense of accidents, it follows also that essence is truly and properly in substances, but is in accidents only in a certain way and in a qualified sense. Some substances indeed are simple, and some are composite. Essence is present in both, but it exists more truly and in a nobler way in simple substances, inasmuch as they have their acts of existing in a nobler way. For simple substances are the cause of composite ones—at least the first substance, God, is. However, because the essences of simple substances are more hidden from us, we must therefore begin with essences of composite ones, so that our study might proceed more suitably from easier things.

Chapter II

In composite substances both the matter and the form[15] are known, as soul and body are known in man. Moreover, neither one of them alone can be called essence. For it is clear that the matter alone of a thing is not its essence, because through its essence a thing both is knowable, and is established in a species and a genus. But matter is neither a principle of knowledge nor that by which something is determined in a genus or species. On the contrary, a thing is so determined by that by which it is in act.[16] Nor can it be

13 Baur and Boyer, *quod per definitionem significatur;* Roland-Gosselin, *quod diffinitionem significat.*

14 Cf. above, *The Principles of Nature,* note 5 (p. 8).

15 Cf. *The Principles of Nature,* chaps. I and II (pp. 7–14).

16 A substantial form actuates matter, thereby making it a certain kind of matter, e.g., human matter. See *The Principles of Nature,* note 5 (p. 8).

said that form alone is the essence of a composite substance, although some [17] try to assert this.

From what we have said, it is evident that essence is that which is signified by the definition of a thing. Moreover, the definition of natural substances contains not only form, but also matter; otherwise there would be no difference between definitions in physics and in mathematics. Nor can it be said that matter is put in the definition of a natural substance as something added to its essence, or as a being outside of its essence, because this kind of definition is proper to accidents, which do not have a perfect essence. Hence the definition of an accident must include its subject, which is outside its genus.

Clearly, then, essence includes matter and form. One cannot, however, say that essence signifies a relationship between matter and form, or something superadded to them, since this would necessarily be an accident or something extraneous to the thing; nor would the thing be known through it. None of these features is suitable for an essence.[18] By form, which is the act of matter, matter is made a being in act and an individual substance. Hence what is superadded does not make matter be in act without qualification, but rather makes matter be actually such, just as accidents do. For example, whiteness makes something be actually white. Accordingly, when such a form is acquired, one says that something is generated in a qualified way,[19] not absolutely.

Consequently, in the case of composite substances, the term "essence" signifies the composite of matter and form. This, too, agrees with Boethius' commentary on the *Categories*,[20] where he says that *ousia* signifies a composite. *Ousia* among the Greeks is the same as *essence* for us, as Boethius himself

[17] See above, note 9 (p. 35). St. Thomas, in *In VII Meta.*, lect. 9, nos. 1467–8, attributes this view to Averroes.

[18] Bauer and Boyer texts read *essentiae non conveniunt;* Roland-Gosselin text omits the *non.* Context seems to demand the former.

[19] See above, *The Principles of Nature*, chap. I (p. 8).

[20] Boethius, *In Categoria* I, in Migne, *Patrologiae cursus completus, Series Latina* (Paris, 1844–1864), Vol. 64, col. 184A.

says in the book *De Duabus Naturis*.[21] Avicenna also says that
the quiddity of composite substances is itself a composition
of form and matter.[22] The Commentator also says in his comment on the seventh book of the *Metaphysics,* "The nature
which species have in things that can be generated is a certain mean, that is, a composite of matter and form." [23] Reason, too, agrees with this, because the existing of a composite
substance is not simply the act of the form alone, nor of
the matter alone, but of the composite itself. Moreover, essence is that according to which a thing is said to be.[24] Hence
it is necessary that an essence, by which a thing is denominated
a being, be neither the form alone nor the matter alone,
but both, although the form in its own way is the cause of
this act of existing. We find the same thing in other things
constituted by a plurality of principles, for a thing gets its
name, not from one or another of these principles alone, but
from what embraces both of them. This is evident in the case
of flavors. Sweetness is caused by the action of heat spreading
moisture. Although heat, in this way, is the cause of sweetness, nevertheless a body is not called sweet because of heat,
but because of flavor, which embraces both heat and moisture.

But, since the principle of individuation is matter,[25] it
might seem to follow that essence, which embraces in itself
both matter and form simultaneously, is particular only and
not universal. From this it would follow that universals would
not have a definition, if essence is that which is signified by
a definition. Accordingly, it should be known that matter in

21 *The Theological Tractates and the Consolation of Philosophy,* chap.
III, p. 89.

22 Avicenna, *Metaphysica,* tr. V, chap. 5F.

23 Averroes, *In VII Meta.,* C. 7, t. c. 27.

24 See above, *The Principles of Nature,* note 5 (p. 8).

25 By "the principle of individuation" is meant that in virtue of which
some particular thing is the singular thing it is. St. Thomas was not always consistent on this matter. Cf. *In I Sent.,* d. VIII, q. 5, a. 2; *In Boet.
de Trin.,* q. IV, a. 2. For a complete review of Aquinas' treatment of this
problem, see M.-D. Roland-Gosselin, *Le "De Ente et Essentia" de S. Thomas
D'Aquin* (Paris: Librarie Philosophique J. Vrin, 1948), pp. 104–126.

just any way is not held to be the principle of individuation. Only designated matter is. By *designated matter* I mean matter considered under determinate dimensions. This matter, however, is not included in the definition of a man insofar as he is a man, but would be included in the definition of Socrates, if Socrates had a definition.[26] Undesignated matter, however, is included in the definition of man. We do not include in man's definition this bone or this flesh, but bone and flesh absolutely, which are the undesignated matter of man. Thus, it is evident that the essence of Socrates and the essence of man differ only in that one is designated and the other is not. Hence the Commentator says in his commentary on the seventh book of the *Metaphysics,* "Socrates is nothing other than animality and rationality, which are his quiddity." [27] So also the essence of a genus and of a species differ according as one is designated and the other not, although a different mode of designation is used in regard to this and to the preceding case, because the designation of an individual with respect to his species is through matter determined by dimensions, whereas the designation of a species with respect to its genus is through a constitutive difference taken from the form of the thing.

However, this determination or designation, which is in the species with respect to the genus, is not through something in the essence of the species that is in no way in the essence of the genus. Rather, whatever is in the species is in the genus in an undetermined fashion. For if *animal* were not the whole

[26] Following Aristotle (*Posterior Analytics* II. 3, 90b30), Aquinas maintains that any singular as such is technically indefinable, inasmuch as every definition is an expression of a concept of an essence (universal) abstracted from a singular thing. This is not to say that the singular cannot be known in its singularity. The intellect, though, must "return to the phantasm," through which the singular is known in its singularity. See St. Thomas, *Summa Theologiae,* II-II, 4, 1c; 9, 2c; *Summa Contra Gentiles,* I, 21. On the intellect's relation to the phantasm, see *Summa Contra Gentiles,* I, 59; *Summa Theologiae,* I, 86, 1c; *De Veritate,* q. 2, a. 6c and ad 3.

[27] Averroes, *In VII Meta.,* 5, t. c. 20.

that is man, but only a part, *animal* would not be predicated of man, since no integral part [28] is predicated of its whole.

How this occurs can be seen if we consider how *body*, understood as part of an animal, differs from *body* understood as a genus. For it is impossible for body to be a genus in the same way as it is an integral part. Therefore this term "body" is understood in many ways. Body is said to be in the genus substance inasmuch as it has a nature such that three dimensions can be designated in it. Indeed, these three designated dimensions themselves are body according as it is in the genus of quantity.

Moreover, it happens in things that what has one perfection may also possess a further perfection. This is evident in man, since he has both a sensitive nature and, beyond that, an intellectual nature. Similarly, to this perfection of having a form such that three dimensions can be designated in it, can be added another perfection, such as life or the like. It is possible, therefore, for this term "body" to signify a certain thing having such a form as there follows precisely and exclusively the capacity of having designated in it three dimensions.[29] Hence from this form no further perfection would follow. If something else were added, it would be outside the meaning of *body* so understood. In this way body is an integral and material part of an animal, because in this

[28] On the problem of the whole and its kinds, see St. Thomas, *Summa Theologiae*, I–II, 17, 4c; *In V Meta.*, lect. 21, nos. 1085–1108; *In IV Phy.*, lect. 4, nos. 435–436.

[29] *Precisione:* Refers to a special way of abstracting. Generally, abstracting is an intellectual operation whereby a real object, e.g., Khrushchev, is known in an incomplete way. To know Khrushchev as human is an act wherein his baldness, obesity, etc., are not considered. However, in such a knowledge of him his individual characteristics are neither positively included nor excluded. Such is abstraction without precision. To form the idea *human nature* from a consideration of him positively excludes his individual features. Such an idea would be formed by abstracting with precision. See St. Thomas, *De Potentia*, V, 9 ad 16. Cf. Joseph Owens, *An Elementary Christian Metaphysics* (Milwaukee: Bruce Publishing Co., 1963), pp. 63–65. In this paragraph Aquinas is speaking of the knowledge of body as an abstraction with precision. In the following paragraph he speaks of it as an abstraction without precision. Cf. below, p. 41.

way soul will be extrinsic to what is signified by the term
"body" and will be an addition to body itself, so that an
animal will be constituted from these two, body and soul, as
from parts.

The term "body" can also mean a certain something having a form such that three dimensions can be designated in
it, whatever that form be, and whether or not a more ultimate
perfection can arise from it. Body in this sense is the genus
animal because nothing is understood in *animal* which is not
contained implicitly in body. For the soul is not another form
distinct from that through which three dimensions can be
designated in that thing. Therefore, when it was said that
body is such that it has a form according to which three dimensions can be designated in it, body was understood, no
matter what form it possesses, whether it be animality, or
rockness, or any other. Thus the form *animal* is contained
implicitly in the form *body,* according as body is its genus.
Such also is the relationship of animal to man. If "animal"
names only a certain thing which has the perfection of sensing
or being moved by a principle existing within it known in
precision [30] from any other perfection, then the addition of
any further perfection would be related to animal as a part,
and not as implicitly contained [31] in the notion of animal. In
this way *animal* would not be a genus. It is a genus insofar
as it signifies anything from whose form can arise sensation
and motion, whatever that form be, whether a sensitive soul
only, or a sensitive and rational one. Therefore, a *genus* signifies indeterminately that whole which is in the species, for
it does not signify matter alone. *Difference* likewise signifies
a whole and does not signify the form alone. A definition,
too, signifies the whole, as does even the species. They do
this, however, in various ways. A genus signifies the whole as
a certain determination, designating what is material in the
thing, exclusive of the determination proper to the form.

[30] See preceding note.

[31] Roland-Gosselin, *contempta;* Baur and Boyer, *contenta,* which was
translated because of the context.

Hence genus is derived from matter, although it is not matter. This is evident from the fact that something is said to be a body from its perfection according to which three dimensions can be designated in it. This perfection is related materially to further perfection. On the other hand, a difference signifies the whole as a certain determination taken determinately from the form, without determinate matter being included in its primary notion. This is evident from the usage of "animate," or that which has a soul, for what this is, whether body or something else, is not determined. Accordingly, Avicenna [32] says that genus is not understood in the difference as part of its essence, but only as a being outside its essence, just as a subject is contained in the understanding of properties. Therefore, too, the genus, properly speaking, is not predicated of the difference, as the Philosopher says in the third book of the *Metaphysics* [33] and in the fourth book of the *Topics*,[34] except perhaps in the way a subject is predicated of a property. But the definition or species includes both, namely, determinate matter, designated by the term "genus," and determinate form, designated by the term "difference."

On the basis of what we have just said, it is clear why genus, species, and difference are related proportionately to matter, form, and the composite in nature, although the former are not the same as the latter. The genus is not matter, but is taken from matter and signifies the whole; and the difference is not the form, but is taken from form as signifying the whole. Accordingly we say that a man is a rational animal, but not that he is composed of animal and rational, as we say that a man is composed of body and soul. For man is said to be composed of body and soul after the manner of a third thing that is constituted of two things, and identical

32 Avicenna, *Metaphysica*, tr. V, chap. 6BC.
33 Aristotle, *Metaphysics* III. 3, 998b24.
34 Aristotle, *Topics* IV. 2, 122b20.

with neither of them.[35] For a man is neither a soul nor a body. However, if man is said to be composed in some way of animal and rational, it is not as a third thing from two other things, but as a third notion from two other notions. For the notion *animal* lacks the determination of a special form which expresses the nature of the thing, inasmuch as animal is matter with respect to the ultimate perfection. However, the notion of this difference, rational, consists in the determination of the special form. The notion of species or definition is constituted from these two notions. Therefore, just as the things which compose are not predicated of the thing composed of them, so neither are constitutive notions predicated of the notion constituted from them. For we do not say that a definition is "genus" or difference.

Although "genus" signifies the whole essence of the species, nevertheless it is not necessary that the diverse species in the same genus have the same essence. This is so because the unity of genus proceeds from its very indetermination or indifference. This is not to say, however, that what is signified by "genus" is numerically one nature in diverse species, to which nature some other thing which is the difference is added, determining it as the form determines matter which is numerically one. It is a question, rather, of "genus" signifying a certain form—not, however, this one or that one determinately. The difference expresses this determinately, and it is none other than the one signified indeterminately by the genus. And this is why the Commentator says in the twelfth book of the *Metaphysics* [36] that prime matter is said to be one through the removal of all forms, whereas genus is said to be one through the community of the form signified. It is

---

[35] In this sentence the word "thing" is used frequently, and is the translation of the Latin word *res*. The reader, however, should be aware that "thing" here is used in a very loose sense, and should not be interpreted to mean a fully constituted being. The whole context indicates that St. Thomas does not maintain that soul, of itself, or body, of itself, is a being. They are principles of being.

[36] Averroes, *In XII Meta.*, 3, t. c. 14.

therefore evident that through the addition of the difference, which thereby removes that indetermination which was the cause of the unity of the genus, essentially diverse species remain.

Now because the nature of the species is, as we have stated,[37] indeterminate with respect to the individual, as is the nature of a genus with respect to the species, it therefore follows that just as a genus, insofar as it is predicated of a species, implies (although indistinctly) in its signification everything determinate in the species, so also the species, as predicated of an individual, must signify (although indistinctly) all that is essentially in the individual. In this way the essence of Socrates is signified by the name "man." Accordingly, *man* is predicated of Socrates. But if the nature of a species is signified in precision [38] from designated matter, which is the principle of individuation, then it will be related to the individual after the manner of a part. In this way the essence of Socrates is signified by the term "humanity." For humanity signifies that whereby man is a man. But designated matter is not that whereby man is a man. Therefore, in no way is designated matter included among those things by which a man is a man. Hence, since humanity includes in its conception only those things by which a man is man, it is clear that designated matter is excluded or precluded from its signification. In addition, since a part is not predicated of the whole, so humanity is predicated of neither man nor Socrates. Accordingly, Avicenna says [39] that the quiddity of a composite is not the composite of which it is the quiddity, even if the quiddity itself is a composite. Hence, although humanity is composite, it is nevertheless not identified with man. Indeed, it must be received in something, which is designated matter.

As has been said,[40] the designation of a species with respect

37 See above, p. 40.
38 See above, note 29 (p. 40).
39 Avicenna, *Metaphysica*, tr. V, chap. 5F.
40 See above, p. 39.

to the genus is through the form, and the designation of an individual with respect to the species is through the matter. Because of this the term signifying that whence the nature of the genus is taken, in precision [41] from the determinate form perfecting the species, must signify the material part of the whole itself, as body is the material part of man. However, the term signifying that whence the nature of the species is taken in precision from designated matter, signifies the formal part.

Therefore, humanity is signified as a certain form, and is said to be the form of the whole—not, however, as something superadded to the essential parts, namely form and matter, as the form *house* is superadded to its integral parts, but rather as a form which is a whole, that is, a form embracing matter. It is, nevertheless, signified in precision from those things according to which matter is apt to be designated. In this way it is clear that the terms "man" and "humanity" signify the essence *man,* but in diverse ways, as has been said.[42] For the term "man" signifies the essence *man* as a whole, inasmuch as it does not prescind from the designation of matter but contains it implicitly and in an indistinct way, just as genus was said [43] to contain the difference. Accordingly, the term "man" is predicated of individuals. The term "humanity," however, signifies the essence *man* as a part, since it contains in its signification only what is in man insofar as he is man, and prescinds from all designation of matter. Hence humanity cannot be predicated of individual men. On account of this, the term "essence" is sometimes predicated of a thing, as when it is said that Socrates is an essence, and sometimes it is denied of a thing, as when it is said that the essence of Socrates is not Socrates.

[41] See above, note 29 (p. 40), for "precision" used here and below.
[42] See above, p. 44. Cf. above, note 29 (p. 40).
[43] *Ibid.*

Chapter III

Having seen, therefore, what is signified in composite substances by the term "essence," we should see how this term is related to the notions of genus, species, and difference. Inasmuch as what belongs to the character *genus, species,* or *difference* is predicated of this designated singular, it is impossible for the character *universal,* namely of a genus or species, to belong to an essence according as it is signified after the manner of a part, as by the term "humanity" or "animality." This is why Avicenna says that rationality is not a difference [44] but the principle of a difference; and by the same token, humanity is not a species, nor is animality a genus. Similarly, it is not possible to say that the character

[44] Avicenna, *Metaphysica,* tr. V, chap. 6A. The problem to which St. Thomas addresses himself in this chapter is the status in being of species, genus, difference, etc.: what reality does, for example, human nature, as such, have? It has come to be known as the "problem of universals." For the medievals the problem was first broached by Porphyry (233–*ca.* 304), a neoplatonist, in his *Isagoge* (an introduction to Aristotle's *Categories*); it was discussed extensively by Boethius, William of Champeaux (*d.* 1121), Peter Abelard (1079–1142), and many others, before and after St. Thomas. In this paragraph Aquinas mentions two solutions. The first, which St. Thomas claims Avicenna rejects, maintains that species, genus, etc., are really existing in singular things. This position, sometimes called exaggerated realism, was held by William of Champeaux, at least until Abelard entered into the famous controversy with him (See Peter Abelard, *The Story of My Misfortunes* [Glencoe: The Free Press, 1958], chap. II; Étienne Gilson, *The Unity of Philosophical Experience* [New York: Scribners, 1947], chap. I). The other solution, mentioned a few lines below, is the so-called Platonic one, which claimed that universals really existed apart from individual instances of them and apart from our knowledge of them. Aristotle claimed Plato held this (See his *Metaphysics* I. 6 and 7, 987a29–988b22; 9, 990b1–991a14). Boethius also seems to have held this. (See his *Theological Tractates and the Consolation of Philosophy,* Bk. V, prose 4, pp. 389–391). There is another solution called nominalism, held by men like Roscelin (*ca.* 1050–*ca.* 1123) and, later, William of Ockham (*d. ca.* 1349), which identified universals with terms, whether mental, spoken, or written, with no foundation at all in reality. Aquinas' solution, sometimes called "moderate realism," and proposed here, maintains universals like the species *man,* which is predicable of many men, has only intentional or mental being, but has a foundation for its formulation in individual men. See his *Quodlibet,* VIII, q. 2, a. 1.

genus and *species* is proper to the essence, where essence is a certain thing existing outside of the singulars, as the Platonists proposed; for then the genus and the species would not be predicated of this individual. One cannot say that Socrates is something separated from himself, nor can one say that what is separated aids in the cognition of this singular. Therefore, we are left with saying that the character *genus* or *species* belongs to an essence according as it is signified as the whole, as by the terms "man" or "animal," insofar as it implicitly and indistinctly contains all that is in the individual.

Nature or essence, understood in this sense, can be considered in two ways. One way is according to its own proper character. This is an absolute consideration of nature. In this way nothing is true of it except what is proper to it as such. Hence the attribution to it of anything belonging to others would be false. As an example, *rational* and *animal,* and whatever else is included in man's definition, are proper to man as man. Neither white nor black, however, nor anything else of this sort which is not in the notion of humanity, belongs to man as man. Accordingly, if the question arises whether the nature so considered can be said to be one or many, neither should be conceded, because each is extrinsic to the notion of humanity, and either can happen to it. For if plurality were included within its notion, the nature *man* could never be one, although it is one insofar as it is in Socrates. Similarly, if unity were included in its notion, then Socrates and Plato would be one and the same, and the nature could not be multiplied in many.

Nature can be considered, however, in another way: according to the act of existing which it has in this or that individual. When so considered, something is predicated of the nature accidentally, in virtue of that in which it exists; it is said, for example, that man is white because Socrates is white. The condition of being white, however, is not proper to man as man.

Now, this nature has two acts of existing: one in singular

things, another in the soul. And according to each, accidents follow upon the aforesaid nature. In addition, the nature, in singulars, has many acts of existing according to the diversity of singulars. Yet according to the first consideration, that is, an absolute one, no act of existing is due the nature. For it is false to say that the essence of man, as man, has the act of existing in this singular inasmuch as, if it were proper to man as man to exist in this singular, man would never exist outside it. Similarly, if it pertained to a man as man not to exist in this singular, then man would never exist in this singular. But it is true to say that is not proper to man as man to exist in this or that singular, or in a soul. It is, therefore, evident that the nature of man considered absolutely abstracts from every act of existing, but in such a way, however, that no act of existing is excluded by way of precision. Now it is this nature so considered which is predicated of all individuals.

Nevertheless, it cannot be said that the character *universal* belongs to nature so understood, because community and unity belong to the character *universal,* whereas neither of these belong to human nature considered absolutely. For if community were included in the notion of man, community would be found whenever humanity was found. But this is false, because in Socrates no community is found. On the contrary, whatever is in him is individuated. Similarly, it cannot be said that the character *genus* or *species* accrues to human nature according as it exists in individuals, because human nature in individuals does not possess such a unity as to be something that is one belonging to all, which the character *universal* demands. It remains, therefore, that the character *species* accrues to human nature as it exists in the intellect. For human nature itself exists in the intellect in abstraction from all individuating conditions. Thus it has a uniform relation to all individuals outside the soul, inasmuch as it is equally the similitude of all and leads to the cognition of all inasmuch as they are men. And since the nature has such a relationship to all individuals, the intellect forms the notion of species [45] and attributes it to the nature. Hence the Commentator says in the first book of the *De Anima* [46] that it is the intellect which makes universality in things. Avicenna makes the same claim in his *Metaphysics*.[47] Hence, although this nature existing in the intellect has the character *universal* inasmuch as it is compared to things which are outside of the mind, since it is the similitude of all of them, nevertheless, according as it exists in this or that intellect, it is a certain particular species understood by the intellect.

For this reason, the defect in the Commentator's reasoning in the third book of the *De Anima* [48] is evident. He chose to conclude to the unity of an intellect for all men from the universality of the known form. This view is defective because the form is not universal according as it exists in the intellect, but inasmuch as it refers to things as their similitude. So also if there were one corporeal statue representing many men, that image or species of the statue would still be properly singular, since it would exist in this matter. It would, however, have the character *community*, inasmuch as it would be the common representation of many.

Since it belongs to human nature absolutely considered to be predicated of Socrates, and since the character *species* does not belong to it absolutely considered, but is among the accidents which follow upon it according as it exists in the intellect, therefore the term "species" is not predicated of Socrates, as in the sentence, "Socrates is a species." This would necessarily happen if the character *species* were proper to man according as it exists in Socrates, or according to its absolute consideration, that is, as man. For whatever belongs to man as man is predicated of Socrates. To be predicated, however,

---

[45] That is, by reflecting upon what has been abstracted from an individual. What has been abstracted thereby acquires the relationship of being predicable of many, i.e., universal.

[46] Averroes, *Commentarium Magnum In Aristotelis De Anima Libros*, ed. F. Stuart Crawford (Cambridge, Mass.: Medieval Academy of America, 1953), Bk. I, com. 8.

[47] Avicenna, *Metaphysica*, tr. V, 1E.

[48] Averroes, *In De An.*, Bk. III, com. 5 and 35.

belongs essentially to genus, since it is posited in the definition of genus. For predication is something which is accomplished by the action of the intellect composing and dividing, and has for its foundation in the real thing itself the unity of those things one of which is said of the other. Hence, the character *predicability* can be included in the nature of this kind of intention, that is, genus, which is similarly accomplished by an act of the intellect. Nonetheless, that to which the intellect attributes the intention *predicability*, composing it with another, is not the intention itself, *genus*. It is rather that to which the intellect attributes the intention *genus*, as the *what* that is signified by this term "animal."

It is evident, therefore, how an essence or nature is related to the character *species*, for the character *species* does not belong to essence or nature considered absolutely, nor is the character *species* one of the accidents which follow upon it according as it exists outside the soul, like whiteness or blackness. The character *species* is included among the accidents which follow upon it according as it exists in the intellect. The characters *genus* and *difference* also belong to nature so considered.

Chapter IV

It now remains for us to see the way in which essence is found in separated substances, namely, the soul, the intelligences,[49] and the First Cause.

Although all hold that the first cause is simple, nevertheless certain men try to introduce a composition of form and matter into intelligences and the soul.[50] Avicebron,[51] the author of the *Fons Vitae*, appears to be the originator of this position. This is contrary to the common views of the philosophers,[52] for they call them substances separated from matter, and prove that they exist without any matter. The strongest argument for this position is from the power of understanding

[49] The word "intelligence" here is synonymous with "angel." See St. Thomas, *Summa Theologiae*, I, 50, 1c.

[50] Generally speaking, this doctrine was common to Aquinas' Franciscan contemporaries, e.g., St. Bonaventure (1221–1274), *In II Sent.*, in *Omnia Opera*, 10 vols. (Florence: Collegii S. Bonaventurae, 1885), dist. 3, pt. 1, a. 1, q. 1, conclu. 3 (Vol. II, p. 91); Roger Bacon (*ca.* 1214–*ca.* 1294), *Liber Primus Communium Naturalium*, in *Opera Hactenus Inedita Rogeri Baconi*, 15 vols. (Oxford: Clarendon Press, 1911), Pt. IV, dist. 3, chap. 4 (Vol. III, pp. 291–294). The positing of some kind of matter in any creature had its source in an attempt to isolate the principle of a finite being's mutability or potentiality. St. Thomas, too, sees each finite being as potential and actual, but finds the potentiality present in virtue of the essence and the actuality in virtue of the act of existing. The Franciscan doctrine is ultimately traceable to St. Augustine. See his *Confessions*, XII, 9; *The City of God*, XII, 15, as found in *Basic Writings of St. Augustine*, ed. and trans. Whitney J. Oates (New York: Random House, 1948), I, 208; II, 194 ff.

[51] Avicebron or Ibn Gabirol, Solomon ben Judah (*ca.* 1021–1058), a Spanish Jewish poet and neoplatonic philosopher. He wrote, however, in Arabic. Reference here is to tr. IV, *Fons Vitae*, translated from the Arabic to Latin (which St. Thomas used) by Johannes Hispanus and Dominicus Gundissalinus, ed. Clemens Baeumker, and found in *Beiträge zur Geschichte der Philosophie des Mittelalters* (Münster: Achendorff-schen, 1895), I, 211 ff.

[52] Certainly Aristotle is intended here. See his *On the Soul* III. 4, 429a10–28. St. Albert the Great (*ca.* 1200–1280) may be intended also. See his *In II Sent.*, in *Omnia Opera* (Paris: Vivès, 1894), d. 1, A, a. 4 (Vol. 27, p. 14).

present in these substances. For we see that forms are actually intelligible only insofar as they are separated from matter and material conditions. Nor can they be made actually intelligible except through the power of an intelligent substance according as they are received in this substance, and are effected through it. It is, therefore, necessary that every substance capable of intellectual understanding be completely free of matter such that it have no matter as part of itself, nor be like a form impressed on matter, as material forms are.[53]

Nor can anyone maintain that not all matter impedes intelligibility, but that only corporeal matter does. If this impeding were of the nature of corporeal matter only, then matter would have to impede intelligibility because of its corporeal form, since matter is not called corporeal except insofar as it exists under a corporeal form. But this is impossible because, like other forms, even a corporeal form is actually intelligible when abstracted from matter. Hence, in no way whatsoever can there be a composition of form and matter in the soul or in an intelligence such that their essence would be understood in the same way as essence in corporeal substances.[54] There is in them, however, a composition of form and act of existing. Wherefore, in the comment on the ninth proposition in the book De Causis,[55] it is said

[53] Aquinas contends here that the forms of singulars are not actually intelligible, inasmuch as each form is united with matter and thereby individualized; hence intellectual cognition requires abstraction. See St. Thomas, *Summa Theologiae,* I, qq. 84 and 85; *De Veritate,* q. 10, a. 6; *Quodlibet,* VIII, q. 2, a. 1. Cf. George Klubertanz, *The Philosophy of Human Nature,* chap. VIII.

[54] For the arguments leading to the conclusion of the soul's spirituality, see references in note 52; see also St. Thomas, *De Anima,* a. 2c.

[55] *Liber de Causis,* an anonymous compilation of extracts from the *Elements of Theology* by Proclus (410–485), a synthesizer of neoplatonic doctrines, especially those of Plotinus (ca. 205–270). The medievals understood the *Liber de Causis* as a kind of commentary, hence Aquinas' phrase "comment on the ninth proposition." See M.-D. Roland-Gosselin, *Le "De Ente et Essentia" de S. Thomas D'Aquin,* III, 146–149; cf. Étienne Gilson, *History of Christian Philosophy in the Middle Ages* (London: Sheed and Ward, 1955), pp. 235–237. See O. Bardenhewer, *Die pseudo-*

that an intelligence is something having form and an act of existing. Form is understood there as the simple quiddity or nature itself.

How this can be so is plain enough. Whatever things are related to each other in such a way that one causes the other to be, that thing which has the nature *cause* can have the act of existing without the other thing, but not vice versa. Such is the relation between matter and form, because form gives existence to matter.[56] It is, therefore, impossible for matter to exist without some form, but it is not impossible for some form to exist without matter. For the form, as form, is not dependent upon matter. However, if some forms are found which can exist only in matter, this happens to them because of their distance [57] from the first principle, which is first and pure act. Accordingly, those forms which are nearest to the first principle are forms subsisting of themselves without matter. As has just been said, form, according to every genus of form, may not need matter; and the intelligences are forms of this kind. Hence, it is not necessary that the essences or quiddities of these substances be other than the form itself. In this, therefore, the essences of composite substances and of simple substances differ, since the essence of a composite substance is not the form alone but includes both form and matter, whereas the essence of a simple substance is the form alone.

This accounts for two other differences. One is that the essence of composite substances can be signified as a whole or as a part. This occurs because of the designation of matter as has just been said. Therefore, not in just any way is the essence of a composite thing predicated of the composite thing itself. For it is not possible to say that a man is his quiddity. But the essence of a simple thing, which is its form, cannot

---

aristotelische Schrift "Ueber das reine Gute" bekannt unter dem Namen "Liber de Causis" (Freiburg, 1882), VIII, 173.

[56] See above, *The Principles of Nature*, note 5 (p. 8).

[57] For a relevant discussion of the term "distance," see below, *On the Virtues in General*, art. XI (p. 105).

be signified except as the whole, since there is nothing in the essence besides the form, as it were to receive the form. Therefore, in whatever way it is taken, the essence of simple substances is predicated of the simple substances. Accordingly, Avicenna says that "the quiddity of simple substances is the simple substance itself,"[58] inasmuch as there is nothing else receiving it.

The second difference is that the essences of composite things, inasmuch as they are received in designated matter, are multiplied according to the division of matter. It happens, therefore, that some are the same in species but different in number. But since the essence of simple substances is not received in matter, no such multiplication is possible. Therefore, among these substances there cannot be many individuals of the same species. Rather, there are as many species as there are individuals, as Avicenna expressly states.[59]

Although substances of this kind are simply forms without matter, nonetheless they are not in every way simple, as pure acts are.[60] They do have an admixture of potency, which is evident in the following way. Whatever is extraneous to the concept of an essence or quiddity is adventitious, and forms a composition with the essence, since no essence can be understood without those things which are its parts. On the other hand, every essence or quiddity can be understood without its act of existing being understood. I can understand what a man or phoenix [61] is, and yet not know whether or not it exists in the nature of things. Therefore, it is evident that the act of existing is other than essence or quiddity. This is true, unless, perhaps, there is something whose quiddity is its very

---

[58] Avicenna, *Metaphysica,* tr. V, 5F.

[59] Avicenna, *Metaphysica,* tr. V, 2A.

[60] God is Pure Act, in the sense that His essence is to be. See above. *The Principles of Nature,* chap. I (pp. 7–10); *De Potentia,* q. 7, a. 2, c and ad 9; *Summa Contra Gentiles,* II, 54; *Summa Theologiae,* I, q. 40, a. 3. Cf. Étienne Gilson, *Being and Some Philosophers,* 2nd edn. (Toronto: Pontifical Institute of Medieval Studies, 1952), V, 154 ff.; cf. also his *Elements of Christian Philosophy* (New York: Doubleday, 1960), pp. 137–203.

[61] A bird described in Egyptian mythology; a symbol of immortality.

act of existing. This thing would have to be unique and primary, since it would be impossible for anything to be multiplied except by the addition of some difference, as the nature *genus* is multiplied into species; or by a form being received in diverse matters, as the nature *species* is multiplied in different individuals; or by one being absolute, and the other being received in something. For example, if there were a certain "separated" heat it would be distinct, in virtue of its very separation from the heat which is not separated. If, however, something is posited which is simply its own act of existing such that it would be subsistent existence itself, this existence cannot receive the addition of a difference, because then it would not be simply an act of existing, but an act of existing plus this certain form. Even less would it receive the addition of matter, because then it would not be subsistent existence, but material existence. Hence, there remains only one such thing that is its own act of existing. Accordingly, in anything other than it, the act of existing must necessarily be other than its quiddity or nature or form. Hence, among the intelligences, their acts of existing must be other than their forms. Therefore, it is said that intelligences are forms and acts of existing.

Whatever belongs to something is either caused by the principles of its nature, like risibility in man, or accrues to it from some extrinsic principle, like the light in the air, which is caused by the sun. It is impossible that the act of existing itself be caused by the form or quiddity—and by "caused" I mean as by an efficient cause—for then something would be the cause of itself and produce itself in existence, which is impossible.[62] It is therefore necessary that everything whose act of existing is other than its nature have its act of existing from another. And because everything which exists through another is reduced to that which exists through itself, as to a first cause, there must be something which causes all

[62] See above, *The Principles of Nature*, note 5 (p. 8). For an extended treatment of causality, see above, *The Principles of Nature*, chaps. III and IV.

things to exist, inasmuch as it is subsistent existence alone. Otherwise we would proceed to infinity in causes,[63] since everything which is not a subsistent act of existing has a cause for its act of existing, as we have just said. It is evident, therefore, that an intelligence is a form and an act of existing, and that it has its act of existing from the First Being which is existence only; and this is the First Cause, God.

Everything that receives something from another is in potency with respect to what is received, and what is received in it is its act. Therefore, that quiddity or form which an intelligence is must be in potency with respect to the act of existing, which it receives from God. And that act of existing is received as an act. Thus potency and act are found in intelligences, but not (except equivocally) matter and form. Hence, even *to suffer, to receive, to be subject to,* and all other things of this kind which seem proper to things in virtue of their matter, belong equivocally to intellectual and corporeal substances, as the Commentator states in his commentary on the third book of the *De Anima.*[64] Likewise, because the quiddity of an intelligence is as has been said,[65] the intelligence itself, its quiddity or essence, therefore, is itself that which is; and its act of existing, received from God, is that by which it subsists in the nature of things. Because of this, certain men [66] contend that a substance of this kind is composed of that by which it is and that which it is, or as Boethius says, of what is and the act of existing.

[63] For a complete exposition of Aquinas' thought on the series of causes, see Gilson, *Elements of Christian Philosophy,* pp. 61–87.

[64] Averroes, *In De An.,* III, 14.

[65] See above, p. 53.

[66] See St. Bonaventure, *In II Sent.,* d. 3, p. 1, a. 1, q. 1, conclu. 1. See also St. Albert the Great, *In II Sent.,* d. 1, A, a. 4. St. Thomas refers in this sentence to Boethius' famous statement, *"Diversum est, tantum esse aliquid, et esse aliquid in eo quod est. . . ."* (*De Hebdomadibus, PL,* Vol. 64, col. 1311C). St. Thomas uses Boethian terminology here, but not Boethian meaning. Boethius understood by *esse* the form by which something is what it is (*quo est*), and by *quod est* a collection of parts reduced to a unity in its possession of the *esse.* See Gilson, *History of Christian Philosophy in the Middle Ages,* pp. 104–105.

Inasmuch as potency and act are found in intelligences, there will be no difficulty in discovering multitude among the intelligences. This would be impossible if there were no potency in them. Hence, the Commentator says in his commentary on the third book of the *De Anima* [67] that if the nature of the possible intellect were unknown to us we could not find multitude in the separated substances. The distinction between them, therefore, is in accordance with the degree of potency and act, such that a superior intelligence which is nearer to the first being would have more act and less potency; and so on with the others. This terminates in the human soul, which holds the lowest grade among intellectual substances. Hence, its possible intellect is related to intelligible forms as prime matter, which holds the lowest grade among sensible beings, is related to sensible forms, as the Commentator says in his commentary on the third book of the *De Anima*.[68] Accordingly, the Philosopher compares it to a writing tablet on which nothing is written,[69] because it has a greater degree of potency than the other intelligible substances. The human soul, then, is so near to material things that the material thing is drawn to participate in its act of existing; thus from body and soul there results one act of existing in one composite, although that act of existing, insofar as it is the soul's, does not depend upon the body.[70] Then, after that form which is the soul,[71] there are other forms having more potency and having a greater propinquity to matter, to the extent that their acts of existing are not without matter. Among these, too, order and grade are found, all the

---

[67] Averroes, *In De An.,* III, 5.

[68] *Ibid.*

[69] Aristotle, *On the Soul* III. 4, 429b31. Cf. St. Thomas, *In III De An.,* lect. 9, no. 722.

[70] Cf. St. Thomas, *De Anima,* q. *unica,* a. 1, c and ad 1. For an outline of Aquinas' views on man, see below, p. 57. Cf. Gilson, *Elements of Christian Philosophy,* pp. 203–219.

[71] Roland-Gosselin text: *que est in anima.* Both Boyer and Baur have *quae est anima* which was translated as context seems to demand.

way down to the primary forms of the elements, which are closest to matter.[72] Hence, they have no operations except in accordance with the demands of their active and passive qualities, and of other qualities by which matter is disposed to form.

Chapter V

From what has been seen previously, it is evident how essence is found in diverse things: for we found among substances a threefold mode of possessing an essence.

There is something, God, Whose essence is its very act of existing. Accordingly, some philosophers [73] argue that God does not have a quiddity or essence because His essence is nothing other than His act of existing. From this it follows that He is not in any genus, since everything that is in a genus necessarily has a quiddity distinct from its act of existing. This, in turn, follows from the fact that the quiddity or nature of a genus or species is not distinguished according to the character *nature* in those things of which there is a genus or species, but according to the act of existing which is diverse in diverse things. If we say that God is only an act of existing, we do not necessarily fall into the error of those [74] who have stated that God is that universal existence by which each thing formally exists. The act of existing which God is is such that no addition can be made to it. Hence, by its very purity, His act of existing is distinct from every other act of existing. A comparable situation would be this: if there were a certain separated color, it would, by its very separation,

[72] See above, *The Principles of Nature,* chap. III (pp. 14–18).

[73] Avicenna, *Metaphysica,* tr. VIII, chap. 4A.

[74] According to Roland-Gosselin (*Le "De Ente et Essentia,"* p. 37, note 2), St. Thomas is referring to Amaury de Bène, an early thirteenth-century professor of theology at the University of Paris. Cf. William of Auvergne (*ca.* 1180–1249), *De Trinitate,* chap. 7, fol. 8b–9a, in *Omnia Opera* (Paris: apud Andraeam Pralaad, 1674; reprint, 2 vols., Frankfort: Minerva, 1963). See also Gilson, *History of Christian Philosophy in the Middle Ages,* pp. 253–255.

be distinct from the color not separated. Wherefore, it is stated in the commentary on the ninth proposition of the book *De Causis* [75] that the individuation of the first cause, which is only an act of existing, is through its pure goodness. However, just as the notion of existing-in-general does not include any addition, neither does it include any precision of addition; for if this were so, nothing in which something were added over and above the act of existing could be understood to exist. Similarly, even though He is only an act of existing, this does not necessitate that He be deficient in other perfections and excellences. Indeed, God possesses the perfections which are in all genera, because of which He is said to be perfect without qualification,[76] as the Philosopher and the Commentator state in the fifth book of the *Metaphysics*.[77] He has these perfections, however, in a more excellent way than other things, because in Him they are one, while in other things they are diverse. This is so because all these perfections belong to Him according to His simple act of existing, just as, if someone were able to perform the operations of all the qualities in virtue of one quality, He would, in that one quality, have all qualities; so God possesses all perfections in His very act of existing.

Essence is found in a second way in created intellectual substances in which their essence is other than their acts of existing, although their essence is without matter. Hence, their acts of existing are not absolute, but received, and, therefore, limited and restricted to the capacity of the receiving nature. Nonetheless, their nature or quiddity is absolute and not received in any matter. Therefore, the book *De Causis* [78] maintains that intelligences are infinite from below and finite from above. For they are limited as to their acts of existing, which

[75] See Bardenhewer, *Die pseudo-aristotelische Schrift. . . ,* VIII, 173.

[76] This follows from Aquinas' view that an essence distinct from the act of existing is a limitation of that act. Hence God, without such a limiting principle, is complete or perfect in the order of being.

[77] Aristotle, *Metaphysics* V. 16, 1021b30. Cf. St. Thomas, *In V Meta.,* lect. 18, nos. 1040–1042. Averroes, *In V Meta.,* 16, t.c. 21.

[78] See Bardenhewer, *Die pseudo-aristotelische Schrift . . . ,* IV, 167.

are received from something higher. They are not limited from below, since their forms are not limited to the capacity of some matter receiving them. Hence, there is not found among such substances a multitude of individuals in one species, as has been said,[79] except in the case of the human soul because of the body to which it is united. And although its individuation depends on the body as the occasion for its beginning, since it does not acquire an individuated act of existing except in the body whose act it is, nevertheless individuation would not necessarily cease if the body were removed. For since the human soul possesses absolutely the act of existing, which is individuated in being received, and from which union the soul is made the form of this body, that act of existing always remains individuated.[80] Accordingly, Avicenna says [81] that the individuation and the multitude of souls depend on the body as to its source, but not on the body as to its end. Moreover, inasmuch as quiddity in these substances is not identical with the act of existing, they can therefore be assigned a category; and because of this, genus, species, and differences are found in them, although the differences proper to them are hidden to us. Even in sensible things essential differences themselves are unknown. They are, therefore, signified through accidental differences which arise from essential ones, just as a cause is signified by its effect; for example, *biped* is proposed as the difference of man. However, the proper accidents of immaterial substances are unknown to us; hence, their differences cannot be signified by us either through themselves or through accidental differences.

One must realize, however, that genus and difference cannot be taken in the same way in these substances and in sensible substances. In sensible substances, genus is taken from what is material in the thing, whereas difference is taken from what is formal in it. Hence Avicenna says in the begin-

[79] See above, p. 54.
[80] Cf. St. Thomas, *Summa Contra Gentiles,* II, 51, 68, 81, and 82.
[81] Avicenna, *De Anima,* in *Opera Philosophica* (Venice, 1508; reprint Louvain: Édition de la Bibliothèque S.J., 1961), p. IV, chap. 3B.

ning of his book *De Anima* [82] that form in things composed of matter and form "is the simple difference of what is constituted from it." This is so not because the form itself is the difference, but rather because it is the principle of the difference, as he states in his *Metaphysics*. [83] Such a difference is called the simple difference, inasmuch as it is taken from that which is a part of the quiddity of the thing—that is, from the form. Moreover, since immaterial substances are simple quiddities, a difference in them cannot be taken from that which is a part of the quiddity, but from the whole quiddity. Therefore, in the beginning of the *De Anima*, [84] Avicenna states that only species whose essence is composed of matter and form have a simple difference. Likewise among them the genus is taken from the whole essence, but in a different way. For one separated substance agrees with the others in immateriality; they differ from each other in grade of perfection according to their withdrawal from potency or approach to pure act. And therefore, a genus among them is taken from what follows upon them inasmuch as they are immaterial, like intellectuality or something of that sort. Their difference, unknown to us, is taken from that which follows in them the grade of perfection.

These differences need not be accidental, because they are according to a greater and a lesser perfection, which do not diversify a species. For a grade of perfection in the reception of the same form does not diversify a species, like being more white or less white in participating in a whiteness of the same nature. A diverse grade of perfection in the participated forms or natures themselves does diversify a species, just as nature advances through grades from plants to animals by way of certain things which are midway between animals and plants, according to the Philosopher in his eighth book of the *De Animalibus*. [85]

The division of intellectual substances, moreover, need not

82 *Ibid.*, p. 1, chap. 1E.
83 Avicenna, *Metaphysica*, tr. V, chap. 5A.
84 Avicenna, *De Anima*, p. I, chap. 1E.
85 Aristotle, *History of Animals* VIII. 1, 588b4–14.

always be through two genuine differences, because this cannot happen in all things, as the Philosopher says in the eleventh book of the *De Animalibus*.[86]

The third way in which an essence is found is in substances composed of matter and form, wherein also the act of existing is received and limited inasmuch as they have it from another, and their nature or quiddity is received in designated matter. Therefore, they are limited from above and from below. Moreover, multiplication of individuals in one species is possible among them because of the division through designated matter. And how essence in these is related to logical intentions has been explained above.[87]

Chapter VI

Having declared how essence is found in all substances, it now remains for us to see how essence is in accidents. As has been said,[88] because essence is what is signified through a definition, accidents must have an essence in the same way that they have a definition. However, they have an incomplete definition, for they cannot be defined except by positing the subject in their definition. This is so because they do not, of themselves, have the act of existing independently of the subject, but, just as a substantial act of existing follows upon a composition of matter and form, so an accidental act of existing follows upon addition of an accident to a subject.[89] Therefore, neither the substantial form itself, nor matter, has a complete essence because in the definition of substantial form one must include that of which it is the form. Thus its definition is through the addition of something extrinsic to

---

[86] Aristotle, *Parts of Animals* I. 2, 642b5.

[87] See above, pp. 44 ff.

[88] See above, p. 37.

[89] Cf. above, *The Principles of Nature,* chap. I (pp. 7–10); cf. St. Thomas, *In VII Meta.,* lect. 4, nos. 1352–1353; *Quodlibet,* IX, a. 3; *Summa Theologiae,* I–II, 110, 2 ad 3.

its class, as is the definition of an accidental form. In the definition of the soul, therefore, the natural philosopher, who considers the soul only insofar as it is the form of the physical body, includes body.

There is, however, this difference between substantial and accidental forms: just as a substantial form does not have through itself an absolute act of existing without that to which it is added, so neither does that to which it is added, namely, matter. Therefore, from their union arises that act of existing in which the thing subsists through itself, and from them is produced something that is one through itself. Hence a certain essence results from their union.[90] Thus, although form, when considered in itself, does not have the complete nature *essence*, nevertheless, it is part of a complete essence. On the other hand, that to which an accident is added is a being complete in itself, subsisting in its own act of existing, which act naturally precedes the added accident. Therefore, an added accident, from its union with that to which it is added, does not cause the act of existing in which the thing subsists and through which the thing is a being through itself; but it does cause a certain second existence, without which the subsisting thing can be understood to exist, as "first" can be understood without "second." Hence, from the union of accident and subject there is not produced something that is one through itself, but something that is accidentally one. And so from their union no distinctive essence results, as results from the union of form and matter. Because of this, an accident neither has the character of a complete essence, nor is part of a complete essence; rather, just as it is a being in a qualified sense, so it has an essence in a qualified sense.

Now what is said maximally and most truly in any genus is the cause of those which are posterior in that genus; for example, fire, which is at the extreme of heat, is the cause of heat in hot things, as is stated in the second book of the *Metaphysics*.[91] Accordingly, substance, which is first in the

---

[90] Cf. above, *The Principles of Nature*, note 5 (p. 8).
[91] Aristotle, *Metaphysics* II. 1, 993b24.

genus *being*, having essence in the truest and fullest sense, must be the cause of accidents, which participate secondarily and in a qualified way in the character of being.

This happens in diverse ways, however. Inasmuch as the parts of a substance are matter and form, certain accidents follow principally upon the form; others, upon the matter. Moreover, there is some form whose act of existing does not depend upon matter, as the intellective soul. Matter, however, has the act of existing only through form. Hence, among the accidents which follow upon form, there is something that does not have any communication with matter, namely, understanding, which does not occur through a corporeal organ, as the Philosopher proves in the third book of the *De Anima*.[92] Indeed, others among those accidents following upon the form do have a communication with matter, as hearing and the like. No accident, however, follows upon the matter without a communication of the form.

There is, moreover, a certain diversity among those accidents which follow upon matter. Certain of them follow upon matter according to an order which they have to a special form; for example, in animals, male and female, whose diversity is reduced to matter, as is stated in the tenth book of the *Metaphysics*.[93] Accordingly, if the animal form is removed, the aforesaid accidents do not remain, except in an equivocal sense. There are others which follow upon matter according to an order which they have to a general form. Hence, if the special form is removed, they nevertheless remain in it, like the blackness of an African's skin, which depends upon a mixture of the elements [94] and not upon the soul. It, therefore, remains in it after death. And because each thing is individuated by matter but is located in a genus or species by its form, accidents which follow upon matter, therefore, are accidents of the individual, according to which individuals of the same species differ from each other. Ac-

[92] Aristotle, *On the Soul* III. 4, 429b4.

[93] Aristotle, *Metaphysics* X. 9, 1058b21.

[94] See above, *The Principles of Nature*, chap. III (pp. 14–18).

cidents which follow the form, however, are proper attributes of the genus or species; hence, they are found in all participants in the nature of the genus or species. For example, risibility follows the form in man, since laughter arises from a certain knowledge in a man's soul.

One should understand likewise that accidents are caused sometimes by the essential principles according to a perfect act, like the heat in fire, which is always actually hot. Sometimes they are caused according to an aptitude only, with completion occurring by the action of an exterior agent; for example, lucency in the air, which is completed by a bright external body. Among these, the aptitude is an inseparable accident, whereas the complement, which comes from some principle which is outside the essence of the thing, or which does not enter into the constitution of the thing, will be separable, as being moved and the like.

It should be known, therefore, that in accidents, genus, species, and difference are understood differently from the way they are understood in substances. For in substances, something that is one through itself is brought about from substantial form and matter, with one certain nature resulting from their union, which properly is placed in the predicament *substance*. Therefore, in substances, concrete names which signify the composite are properly said to be in the genus, as a species or genus; for example, *man* or *animal*. However, neither the form nor the matter is in the predicament in this way except by reduction, as a principle is said to be in a genus. But something that is one through itself does not come about from the union of accident and subject. Hence, from their union there does not result any nature to which the intention *genus* or *species* can be attributed. Accordingly, accidental names said concretely, like *white* and *musical*, are not placed in a category, as species or genus are, except by reduction. They are placed in a category only according as they are signified abstractly, like *whiteness* or *music*.

In addition, because accidents are not composed of matter and form, genus in them cannot be taken from matter, nor difference from form, as in composite substances. Their first genus must be taken from the very mode of existing, according as *being* is said diversely,[95] with certain priorities and posteriorities, of the ten genera of predicaments. Accordingly, quantity is called being inasmuch as it is the measure of a substance; quality, insofar as it is a disposition of a substance; and so on for the others, as the Philosopher says in the fourth book of the *Metaphysics*.[96] On the other hand, differences in accidents are taken from the diversity of the principles by which they are caused. So, because proper attributes are caused by the proper principles of the subject, the subject, therefore, is included in their definition in place of a difference. This is true if they are defined in any absolute way, according as they are properly in a genus; for example, it is said that snubness is curvature of the nose. But the converse is true, if their definition is taken according as they are said concretely. Then a subject is placed in their definition as a genus, since then they would be defined after the manner of composite substances wherein the character genus is taken from matter. Accordingly, we say that a snub nose is a curved nose. The same is true if one accident is the principle of another accident, as action, passion, and quantity are the principles of relation. Therefore, in the fifth book of his *Metaphysics*,[97] the Philosopher divides relation according to this. But because the proper principles of accidents are not always evident, we sometimes take the differences of accidents from their effects; for example, *contractive* and *expansive* are called differences of color, and are caused by the abundance or scarcity of light which produce diverse species of color.[98]

---

[95] Being, for Aquinas, is predicated analogously. See above, *The Principles of Nature*, chap. VI (pp. 26–28).

[96] Aristotle, *Metaphysics* IV. 2, 1003a33–b10.

[97] Aristotle, *Metaphysics* V. 15, 1020b26 ff.

[98] Color for St. Thomas, following Aristotle, was a species of the genus *sense quality*, and had two contraries, white and black, between which all other colors were situated. These other colors were thought

It is evident, therefore, how essence is found in substances and in accidents, in composite substances and in simple substances, and how universal intentions of logic are found in all these. An exception was made, however, of the first principle, which is the ultimate in simplicity, and to which, because of its simplicity, the character *genus, species,* and consequently *definition,* does not belong. This brings us to the end and consummation of this discourse.

---

to be a mixture of various combinations of the contraries. White was thought to expand vision, i.e., allow one to see best, while black contracted vision. The closer an intermediate color was to white, the more it expanded vision. Accordingly, colors were not distinguished by what they are in themselves, but by what they do, i.e., their effect of expanding or contracting vision. See Aristotle, *De Anima* II. 10, 442a23–25; *Metaphysics* X. 7, 1057b1–34. See also St. Thomas, *In de Sensu et Sensato,* lect. 11, no. 152; *In X Meta.,* lect. 3, no. 1968; lect. 9, nos. 2106–2107. Cf. F. Birren, *Color: From Ancient Mysticism to Modern Science* (New York: University Books, Inc., 1963), pp. 67–69.

On the Virtues in General

Introduction to
On the Virtues in General

The reader will recall from the General Introduction to this volume that the usual manner of teaching during the thirteenth century was a dialectical one, in which a precise question was raised, and the opinions of authorities on the question examined; this was followed by the master's proposing his own solution to the problem, along with his reasons for this solution, and finally, the authoritative opinions were reconsidered in the light of the master's position. The two treatises that we have seen so far, *The Principles of Nature* and *On Being and Essence,* were written by St. Thomas when he was still in his graduate studies at the University of Paris—that is, sometime before 1256, when he became a Master of Theology. Accordingly, neither of these treatises takes the form of a dialectical consideration of a problem; however, the next two treatises, written after 1256, are dialectical in character. They are, therefore, either summaries of dialectical discussions (disputations) that were actually held in a lecture hall, or perhaps even compositions written apart from any actual and immediate classroom discussion, but couched in the form of the dialectical procedure.

It should be noted likewise that while the treatises as we possess them are composed of a number of articles, it is not necessarily true that St. Thomas sat down and wrote each of the articles in their present order. Rather, this order may be the work of some later editor of the Latin manuscripts who assembled the articles. In some disputations, such as the *De Malo,* certain articles are obviously out of place. Accordingly, scholars are reluctant to maintain that the sequence and arrangement of the articles are as St. Thomas composed them.

I have not incorporated into this translation the first and last parts of the articles—that is, those sections dealing explicitly and primarily with the views of recognized authorities. While these may occasionally be of help to advanced students of Thomistic studies, they frequently tend to obscure the body of the article, which contains the real thought of St. Thomas.

To appreciate St. Thomas' views on virtue and the virtues, one must have grasped some of his fundamental conceptions of man. Considered as a being, man is composite, possessing an act of existing, a substantial form, a principle of prime matter, and numerous accidental principles. Each of these metaphysical principles is discussed in the two previous treatises. Virtue can be considered only in the light of the whole framework of man's composition.

Perhaps the best way to introduce the reader to the Thomistic philosophy of man is through the principle *agere sequitur esse*—that is, "action follows being." So much hinges on this that it might be called a Thomistic first principle. Through it Aquinas is saying that action necessarily follows from existence. Inasmuch as there is something existing, there is, and must be, action; and the type of action this something performs is determined by the type of being it is. As we saw in both the previous treatises, the kind of being a being is, is determined ultimately by its form. Hence form determines what a being is and its kind of activity. In the light of this, moreover, form determines the end or goal in activity, since it determines that of which a being is capable.

Furthermore, living things are called living insofar as they perform what might be called vital actions, like growth and reproduction. Now Aquinas (who incidentally is following Aristotle) retains the same view with regard to the determinant of actions in a living thing as he does in an inanimate thing. The form of a living thing determines its mode of activity. However, inasmuch as a living thing's form allows for vital actions, that form has a special name—that is, soul.

As form, then, soul determines for the being what kind of

action it can perform. However, St. Thomas maintains that soul is not the immediate determinant; he maintains that actions flow immediately from powers or faculties such as the intellect, the will, or the sense of sight. While the power immediately determines a type of action the form determines which powers a substance will possess. Accordingly, a man thinks because he has an intellect, and he possesses an intellect because he has a human form or soul.

One further step takes us to Aquinas' theory of virtue. It is obvious that the intellect of one man—a mathematician, for example—can be modified or trained to think efficiently, easily, and with some pleasure about a certain kind of object. The same is true with respect to certain moral areas. Some men can discipline themselves in such a way that we can refer to them as just, or temperate, or courageous. Now it is Aquinas' contention that such intellectual or moral features of a person are real qualities which inhere in certain of his powers or faculties and which affect their functioning. These qualities are called habits. If they are good habits, they are virtues; if bad, they are vices.

Finally, one should be aware of the ontological status of virtue, as conceived by Aquinas. The terms "virtue" and "virtuous" are usually taken to have an operational meaning. Accordingly, when it is said, for example, that John is courageous, such a statement is usually interpreted to mean that John acts in a certain way under certain conditions. By contrast, St. Thomas would interpret such a statement to mean that John is existing in a certain way, that is, possessed of a certain quality. This quality, indeed, affects John's actions, but the virtue is constituted by the inhering quality.

There are four powers that are the subjects of virtue: intellect, will, the concupiscible appetite, and the irascible appetite. The reader will find detailed descriptions of these powers in the treatise. It is sufficient to say here that the intellect is the power by which man knows; the will a power by which man chooses; the concupiscible and irascible appetites powers by which man has emotions, like taking pleasure in food or sex, or simply getting angry. The point is that virtue is not confined to what might be called the moral areas. The intellect can be the subject of virtue, a quality or qualities through which its act of knowing can be improved.

In addition to establishing the nature of virtue and enumerating and describing the basic kinds of virtue, St. Thomas also integrates into his theory of virtue some specifically theological topics, especially that of grace. The reader should not be surprised at this in the light of St. Thomas' goal of faith seeking understanding, and also in the light of his desire to be concrete rather than abstract. A purely natural man is an abstraction, or even a fiction. Every man is in a state either of sin or of grace, and any treatise on virtue that ignored this would amount to a gross misrepresentation of the status of real men.

The text printed in the Marietti manual series, published in Turin, was the one translated.

On the Virtues In General

Article I
Whether the Virtues Are Habits

REPLY: It must be said that *virtue,* according to the meaning of the name, designates the complement of a potency.[1] Wherefore it is also called *power,* according as a certain thing, through the completed potency it has, can follow its impetus or motion. The name "virtue" indicates the perfection of a power, and hence the Philosopher states in the first book of *On the Heavens and Earth* [2] that virtue is the ultimate perfection of a potency. Because a potency is spoken about in reference to act, the complement of a potency refers to what accounts for perfect operation. Because operation is the end of the one who acts—since everything, according to the Philosopher in the first book *On the Heavens and Earth,*[3] exists for the sake of its operation as for its proximate end [4]— each thing is good according as it has a complete ordination to its end. It is in accordance with this that virtue makes its possessor good and his work good, as is said in the second

1 The Latin word *potentia,* rendered "potency" in the text, has in St. Thomas' writings two meanings. Basically, any potency is a capacity for something. The capacity may be to exist in a certain way, as plaster has the capacity for paint. On the other hand, the capacity may be to perform an operation, as man has the capacity to think. The former is a purely passive potency, whereas the latter is an active potency. The word *potestas,* used a few lines below, is equivalent to active potency. The term *vis,* rendered "power," designates a *potestas* which has been perfected, as a man's capacity to make tools has been perfected through experience. Virtue, finally, names the perfection of the *potestas.* See St. Thomas, *Summa Contra Gentiles,* II, 25; *De Potentia,* q. 1, a. 1.

2 Aristotle, *On the Heavens* I. 11, 281a6–25.

3 *Ibid.,* 8, 276a22–29.

4 See St. Thomas, *Summa Theologiae,* I, 105, 5c; I–II, 3, 2c.

book of the *Ethics*.[5] Also in accordance with this, it is evident
that virtue is a disposition of something perfect to the best,
as is said in the seventh book of the *Metaphysics*.[6]

All these things are proper to the virtue of anything. For
the virtue of a horse is what makes it and its work good. A
similar situation holds for the virtue of a rock, or a man, or
any other thing.

The mode of a virtue's combination with a potency is
diverse, according to the diverse condition of potencies. For
some potencies are active only, whereas others are passive
only, and still others are both active and passive.

A potency, therefore, which is active only need not be
moved to be a principle of activity. Hence the virtue of such
potency is nothing other than the potency itself. Such potencies
are the divine potencies,[7] the agent intellect,[8] and natural
potencies.[9] Hence, the virtues of these potencies are not
habits, but the very potencies complete in themselves.

Those potencies are passive only which act only when
moved by others. It is not up to these to act or not to act,
but they act according to the impetus of the moving power.
Such are the sensitive powers considered in themselves. It
is said, therefore, in the third book of the *Ethics*,[10] that sense
is the principle of no act. These powers are perfected in their
acts by something superadded which is not intrinsic to them,
like a certain form remaining in the subject, but only in the
manner of a passion, like a species in the pupil of the eye.
Hence, the virtues of these potencies are not habits, either.
Rather, the potencies themselves are their own virtues according as they are put into act by their movers.

5 Aristotle, *Nicomachean Ethics* II. 6, 1106a15–17.

6 Aristotle, *Metaphysics* VII. 4, 1029b5–6.

7 On the notion of divine potencies, see St. Thomas, *De Potentia*, q.
1, a. 1.

8 See above, *On Being and Essence*, note 51 (p. 51); *Quodlibet*, VIII, q.
2, a. 1.

9 On powers of things of nature, see St. Thomas, *Summa Theologiae*,
I–II, 55, 1c; *De Veritate*, I, 9c.

10 Aristotle, *Nicomachean Ethics* III. 1, 1110a1–4.

Those potencies are active and passive which are so moved by their movers that they are not, however, determined by them to one kind of activity. Rather, it belongs to these potencies to act, as, for example, powers that are in some way rational. These powers are completed with respect to their action by something superadded which is not in them in the manner of a passion only, but by way of a form which remains and continues in the subject. The potency, however, is not necessarily determined to one act by the form, for then the potency would not have dominion over its act. The virtues of these potencies are not the potencies themselves, nor are they the passions, as is the case in sense powers, nor are they qualities acting of necessity, as are the qualities of natural things. Rather, they are habits according to which someone can act when he wills, as the Commentator says in the third book of the *On the Soul*.[11] Augustine, moreover, says in the book *De Bono Coniugali*[12] that a habit is that by which someone acts when the time is appropriate.

It is evident, therefore, that virtues are habits. Moreover, it is manifest how a habit is distinct from the second and third species of quality,[13] and differs, moreover, from the fourth species, for figure of itself does not bespeak an ordering to act.

From what has been said it is possible to show that three things are needed for habits to be virtues. First, there must be a uniformity in their operation. For those things which are dependent on operation alone are easily changed, unless they are rendered stable by some habitual inclination. Second, perfect operation must be performed readily. For, unless a rational potency be in some way inclined to one by a habit, it will always be necessary, when action is demanded, to in-

11 Averroes, *In De An.*, III, 18.

12 Augustine, *De Bono Coniugali*, *Corpus Scriptorum Ecclesiasticorum Latinorum*, ed. Joseph Zycha (Vienna: F. Tempsky, 1866–1957), XLI, 219.

13 Aristotle contended there are four kinds (species) of quality: (1) habit and disposition; (2) capacity or incapacity; (3) sense quality; (4) form and figure. See Aristotle, *Categories* VIII. 8, 8b25–10a24.

quire about the operation. This is evident in him who wishes to speculate but does not yet have the habit of science. It is also evident in him who wishes to act virtuously but who lacks a virtuous habit. Hence, the Philosopher says in the fifth book of the *Ethics* [14] that the actions done out of habit are done quickly. Third, the perfect operation must be completed pleasurably. This indeed occurs through a habit. Since a habit is in the manner of a certain nature, it renders the operation proper to itself almost natural and, consequently, delectable. For agreeableness is the cause of pleasure. Hence the Philosopher, in the second book of the *Ethics*,[15] proposes pleasure in operation as the sign of a habit.

Article II

Whether Augustine's Definition of Virtue Is a Suitable One, Namely, Virtue Is a Good Quality of the Mind by Which One Lives Rightly, Which No One Uses Badly, and Which God Produces in Us Without Us

REPLY: It must be said that this definition of virtue is complete—even with the last portion omitted—and, moreover, proper to every human virtue.

As has been said,[16] a virtue perfects a potency with respect to perfect act. For perfect act is the end of a potency or of the one who acts. Hence, a virtue makes both the potency and the one who acts good, as has been said previously.[17] Therefore, one must posit in the definition of virtue something which pertains to the perfection of the act, and something which pertains to the perfection of the potency or of the one who acts.

[14] Aristotle, *Nicomachean Ethics* V. 1, 1129a6.
[15] *Ibid.*, II. 3, 1104b4.
[16] See above, p. 75.
[17] *Ibid.*

Two things, however, are required for the perfection of an act. The act must be right, and the habit cannot be the principle of a contrary act. For that which is the principle of both good and evil action cannot, as such, be the perfect principle of a good act, since a habit is the perfection of a potency. Such a principle of a good act cannot in any way be the principle of an evil act. On account of this the Philosopher says in the sixth book of the *Ethics* [18] that opinion, which can be true and false, is not a virtue, but that science, which deals in nothing but the true,[19] is a virtue. The first of the requirements is designated by the words "by which one lives rightly"; the second, by the words "which no one uses in an evil way."

Three things must be considered when we talk about virtue making a subject good. One is the subject itself, and this is indicated by the word "mind," for a virtue cannot be human except in what belongs to man as man. The perfection of the intellect is indicated by the word "good," for good is said according to an order to an end.[20] Finally, the mode of inherence is indicated by the word "quality," [21] for virtue cannot inhere as a passion, but as a habit, as has been said above.[22]

All these things belong to both moral and intellectual virtue, to theological virtue,[23] to acquired virtue, and to infused virtue. Augustine's additional phrase, though, "which God produces in us without us," belongs only to infused virtue.

[18] Aristotle, *Nicomachean Ethics* VI. 5–6, 1140b25–33.

[19] One usually thinks of virtue in a moral sense. Aristotle and Aquinas, however, attached a broader meaning to the term. For them a perfected intellectual ability is a virtue, as are qualities in the moral sense. See below, arts. VI and VII (pp. 86–91).

[20] On the notion of the good, see St. Thomas, *Summa Theologiae*, I, q. 5, *passim;* I, 16, 1c; *Summa Contra Gentiles*, I, 37 and 39. Cf. Aristotle, *Nicomachean Ethics* I. 1, 1094a2–3.

[21] See above, note 13 (p. 77).

[22] See above, p. 77.

[23] See below, art. X (pp. 99–102).

Article III

Whether a Potency of the Soul Can Be the Subject of a Virtue

REPLY: It must be said that a subject is related in three ways to an accident.[24]

In the first way as providing a foundation for it; for an accident does not subsist of itself, but rather is upheld through a subject. In another way, as potency to act; for a subject is subject to an accident as a certain potency for what is active. Hence, an accident is called a form. In the third way, as a cause to an effect.[25] For subject-principles are of themselves principles of accidents.

In regard to the first, therefore, one accident cannot be the subject of another. For since no accident subsists of itself, it cannot provide a foundation for another—except, perhaps, in the sense that supported by a subject, it supports another accident.

With regard to the other two ways, however, one accident is related to another as a subject. For one accident is in potency to another, as transparency is to light and as a surface is to color. One accident can even cause another, as moisture causes flavor. It is in this way that one accident is said to be the subject of another accident: not that one accident can provide a foundation for another, but that a subject receives one accident through the mediation of another. In this way a potency of the soul is said to be the subject of habit.

A habit is related to a power of a soul as act to potency. For, since a potency of itself is indeterminate, it is determined by habit to this or that. And acquired habits are caused by the principles of potencies. Therefore, it must be said that powers

24 See above, *On Being and Essence*, chap. VI (pp. 52–57).

25 "Cause" and "effect" are used in a number of different ways by St. Thomas. See above, *The Principles of Nature*, chaps. III and IV (pp. 14–23).

are the subjects of virtues, because a virtue is in a soul through the mediation of a power.

Article IV

Whether the Irascible and Concupiscible Appetite Can Be Subjects of Virtue

REPLY: It must be said concerning this question that there is partial agreement among all. On the other hand, the opinions are partly incompatible.

All concede that some virtues exist in the concupiscible and irascible appetites [26]—for instance, temperance in the concupiscible and fortitude in the irascible. The difference in opinion lies in the following.

Certain men [27] distinguish a double irascible, and a double concupiscible, appetite: one in the superior, and one in the inferior, part of the soul. They maintain that inasmuch as the irascible and concupiscible appetites in the superior part pertain to rational nature, they can be subjects of virtue. This, however, is not true of those appetites in the inferior part of the soul, which pertain to the sensuous and brute nature. This problem is taken up in another question, namely, whether in the higher part of the soul two powers, the iras-

---

[26] The concupiscible and irascible appetites are two sensory powers of the soul whose acts are conscious tendencies. The former has as its object something pleasurable, such as a tasty apple. The desire a man might feel for such an apple has its source in the concupiscible appetite. The latter has as its object the difficult good, such as a college degree. The aggression or "push" which a student might feel toward such an object has its source in the irascible appetite. See St. Thomas, *De Veritate,* q. 25, aa. 1–7; *Summa Theologiae,* I., q. 81, aa. 1–3.

[27] In his *Summa Theologiae,* I, 82, 5, and in his *De Veritate,* q. 25, a. 3, St. Thomas takes up the problem of whether concupiscible and irascible actions are functions of the will. The problem arises since it appears that fear, anger, and desire for sensuous pleasure are actions of the will. In these considerations St. Augustine seems to be the individual whom Aquinas has in mind as having maintained a twofold distinction in the concupiscible and irascible appetite.

cible and the concupiscible,[28] can, properly speaking, be distinguished. But no matter what is said in regard to this question, it is nonetheless necessary to posit some virtues in the concupiscible and irascible powers of the inferior appetite. This accords with the Philosopher's view in the third book of the *Ethics*.[29] Others also make this claim. The necessity is evident from the following.

Since a virtue, as stated above,[30] names a certain complement of a potency, and since a potency, moreover, is related to an act, human virtue must be posited in that potency which is the principle of human acts. But not every act exercised in or by a man is called "human," since there are certain actions which plants, brutes, and men all have in common. A human act is an act which is proper to man. Among other things, moreover, this is proper to man in his act, namely, that he has dominion over it. Any act over which man is master is properly a human act. Those, however, over which man does not have dominion, like digesting or growing, and the like, although they occur in man, are not human acts. Therefore, human virtue can be posited in that which is the principle of that act over which man does have dominion.

Nevertheless, it must be understood that a threefold principle is involved in an act of this sort. The first is the primary moving and ordering force through which man has dominion over his act: his reason or will. The second is a moved mover, the sensible appetite,[31] which is moved by the superior appetite,[32] inasmuch as it is obedient to it, and in turn moves the exterior members by its own command. The third is that which is moved only, namely, an exterior member.[33]

---

[28] See St. Thomas, *De Veritate*, q. 25, a. 3; *Summa Theologiae*, I, 59, 4; q. 82, a. 5.

[29] Aristotle, *Nicomachean Ethics* III. 6–12, 1115a8–1119b20.

[30] See above, p. 75.

[31] Either the concupiscible or the irascible appetite, or both.

[32] The human will.

[33] Any physical part of the body over which man has some control, such as hands, feet, etc.

Although both exterior member and inferior appetite are moved by the superior part of the soul, one is moved in one way and the other in another. An exterior member unresistingly obeys the command of the superior without any repugnance according to the order of nature—if, of course, there is no impediment. This is evident in the movement of our hands and feet. However, an inferior appetite has a proper inclination from its nature. Hence, it does not unresistingly obey the command of the superior appetite, but occasionally offers resistance. Accordingly, Aristotle says in his *Politics*[34] that the soul rules the body despotically, as a ruler dominates a servant who does not have the faculty of resisting any command of the ruler. Reason, however, rules the inferior parts of the soul with regal and political dominion, that is, as kings and leaders of states rule free men who have the right and the faculty of resisting some precepts of the king or leader.

Therefore, nothing perfective of the human act is needed in the exterior member except its natural disposition through which it is apt to be moved by reason.

But in the inferior appetite, which can resist reason, something is needed by which the operation that reason commands will be executed without resistance. For if the immediate principle of an operation is imperfect, the operation necessarily will be imperfect, no matter how perfect the superior principle is. Therefore, if the inferior appetite is not perfectly disposed to follow the command of reason, the operation which is from the inferior appetite as from a proximate principle will not be perfect in goodness. For the operation will involve a certain resistance on the part of the sensible appetite; from this a certain sadness will follow in the inferior appetite, moved with a kind of violence by the superior appetite. This happens in a man who has strong movements of concupiscence which, nevertheless, are not followed because of the prohibition of reason.

Therefore, whenever a man's operation is concerned with the objects of the sensible appetite, the goodness of the

34 Aristotle, *Politics* I. 5, 1254b3–4.

operation requires that a certain disposition or perfection be present in that appetite, through which it might obey reason with facility. We call this disposition a virtue.

When, therefore, a certain virtue concerns those things which properly pertain to the irascible power, like fortitude with respect to fears and bold acts, or optimism with respect to things which are difficult to hope for, or gentleness with respect to annoying things, such a virtue is said to be in the irascible appetite as in a subject. When, on the other hand, a certain virtue concerns itself with those things which are proper to the concupiscible appetite, this virtue is said to be in the concupiscible appetite as in a subject: for example, chastity, which concerns itself with sexual pleasures, and sobriety and abstinence, which concern themselves with the pleasures of food and drink.

Article V

Whether the Will Is a Subject of Virtue

REPLY: It must be said that through a habit of virtue, a potency subjected to it acquires a complement with respect to its act. Hence, the habit of virtue is not necessary for that to which a potency extends itself by its very nature. Virtue orders potencies to the good, for by it the one having the virtue is made good, as is his operation.

The will, by the very nature of its potency, has that which virtue produces in other potencies, for its object is the good. Hence, tending to the good is related to the will, as tending to something pleasurable is related to the concupiscible appetite, and being ordered to sound is related to the sense of hearing. Hence the will needs no habit of virtue to incline it to the good proportioned to it, because it tends to this by the very nature of its potency. But it does need a habit of virtue to tend to that good which transcends the capacity of its potency.

Since anyone's appetite tends to a good proper to the one

who tends, a good can exceed the capacity of the will in two ways: in one way by reason of species, in another by reason of the individual. A good is excessive by reason of species when the will is elevated to some good which exceeds the limits of human good. By "human" I mean that of which man is capable by his natural powers. But the divine good is beyond the human good. Man's will is elevated to the divine good by charity, and also by hope.[35]

A good is excessive by reason of the individual when someone seeks the good of another, although in this case the will is not borne beyond the limits of human good. Thus justice perfects the will, as do all virtues involving a tendency to something other, like liberality [36] and others of the same kind. For justice concerns the good of another, as the Philosopher says in the fifth book of the *Ethics*.[37]

Therefore, two virtues, namely charity and justice, exist in the will as in a subject. And a sign of this is that these virtues, although they pertain to the appetitive, nevertheless do not depend on the passions, as do temperance and fortitude. Accordingly, it is evident that they are not in the sensitive appetite where passions are found, but in the rational appetite—the will—where there are no passions. For every passion is in the sensitive part of the soul, as proved in the seventh book of the *Physics*.[38] Those virtues which depend on the passions, like fortitude in relation to fears and movements of boldness, and temperance in relation to the movements of concupiscence, must for the same reason be in the sensitive appetite. Nor is it necessary, by reason of these passions, for the will to possess any virtue, since the good involved in these passions is according to reason. And the will, by reason of its

---

35 St. Thomas speaks here of the infused virtues of charity and hope. See below, art. X (pp. 99–102).

36 A species of the virtue of justice, through which its possessor tends to be generous to others with his possessions. See St. Thomas, *Summa Theologiae*, II–II, 117, 2. Cf. Aristotle, *Nicomachean Ethics* IV. 1, 1119b20–1120a4.

37 *Ibid.*, V. 1, 1130a4–5.

38 Aristotle, *Physics* VII. 2, 244b11–12.

very potency, is naturally related to this good, since it is the proper object of the will.

Article VI

Whether the Practical Intellect[39] Is the Subject of Any Virtue

REPLY: It must be said that the difference between natural virtues and rational virtues is that a natural virtue is determined to one, while a rational virtue is related to many.

Moreover, an animal or rational appetite must be inclined to its appetible object by some prior cognition. For an inclination to an end without prior knowledge pertains to a natural appetite, as something heavy is inclined to the middle. But inasmuch as some apprehended good must be the object of a rational or animal appetite, therefore wherever this good is uniform, there can be a natural inclination in the appetite and a natural judgment in the cognitive power,[40] as happens in brutes. Since they have few operations because of the debility of their active principle, which extends to only a few things, each member of a species is related to a uniform good. Hence, they tend to it by a natural appetite, and make natural judgments about that proper good, through a cognitive power. It is by such natural judgment and appetite that every swallow uniformly builds his nest and every spider spins his web. The same observation can be made in all other brutes.

Man, however, has many diverse operations, because of the nobility of his active principle, namely, the soul, whose power extends in a certain way to an infinite number of things.[41]

---

39 St. Thomas speaks of both a practical and a speculative intellect. The terms actually refer to the same power but are used to refer to different functions of that power. See St. Thomas, *Summa Theologiae,* I, 14, 16c; I, 79, 11c; *De Veritate,* q. 3, aa. 2-3.

40 See St. Thomas, *Summa Theologiae,* I, 78, 4c; *De An.,* q. *unica,* a. 13c; *De Veritate,* q. 14, a. 1 ad 9.

41 In the sense primarily of the soul's ability through the intellect to know in some way everything. St. Thomas contends that the object of the intellect is being. See his *Summa Theologiae,* I, 78, 1c; 79, 2c.

Therefore, a natural appetite for the good would not be sufficient for man to act rightly; nor would a natural judgment, unless it were more fully determined and perfected.

Indeed, man is inclined to seek his proper good through a natural appetite, but since this varies in many ways and the good of man consists in many things, a natural appetite in man for this determinate good is impossible because of all the conditions which are required for this to be good for him, for this varies in many ways according to diverse conditions of persons, times, places, and the like.

The same reasoning holds for natural judgment, which is uniform. It would not suffice for the pursuit of a good of this sort. Accordingly, through the use of his reason, which is capable of comparing diverse things, man must find and judge his proper good, determined according to all the conditions insofar as his proper good must be sought here and now. For reason to do this without a perfecting habit would be like reason in the speculative order trying to judge a conclusion of some science without having the habit of that science. This, of course, could only be done imperfectly and with a good deal of difficulty.

Therefore, just as it is necessary for the speculative reason [42] to be perfected by the habit of science in order to make correct judgments about knowable things pertaining to some science, so it is necessary for the practical reason to be perfected by some habit in order to judge rightly about the human good in singular actions. This virtue is called "prudence" and its subject is the practical reason. It perfects all the moral virtues in the appetitive part, each one of which inclines the appetite to some kind of human good. Thus, justice inclines one to the good of equality among those things conducive to human well-being; temperance inclines one to the good of restraining the movements of concupiscence, and so on with each virtue.

---

[42] The nouns "reason" and "intellect" refer to one and the same power, but carry different connotations. See St. Thomas, *Summa Theologiae*, I, 79, 8; *De Veritate*, q. 15, a. 1.

Each one of these goods can be brought about in many ways, and not in the same way for all men. Hence, to establish the right way of acting, a prudence of judgment is required. Accordingly, thanks to prudence, there is a rectitude and complement of goodness in all the other virtues. Hence, the Philosopher says [43] that the mean in moral virtue is determined by right reason. Since all habits of an appetitive power share in the character *virtue* thanks to this rectitude and this complement in goodness, it follows that prudence is the cause of all the virtues of the appetitive part, and they are called "moral" insofar as they are virtues. For this reason, Gregory says in Book Twenty-Two of his *Moralia* [44] that the other virtues can never be virtues unless the things they pursue are pursued prudently.

Article VII

Whether There Is Any Virtue in the Speculative Intellect

REPLY: It must be said that in any one thing *virtue* is said in relationship to good, inasmuch as virtue is what makes its possessor good and renders his operation good, as the Philosopher says in Book Two of the *Ethics*.[45] For example, the virtue of a horse makes it be a good horse, run well, and carry his rider well—which is the work of a horse. From this it therefore follows that any habit will have the character *virtue* inasmuch as it directs one to a good.

[43] Aristotle, *Nicomachean Ethics* II. 6, 1107a1–3.

[44] St. Gregory I, or Gregory the Great (*ca.* 540–604), a member of a Roman patrician family who joined the monastic Benedictines, and later was acclaimed pope. Gregory was influential in the problems of papal vs. secular authority, and of clerical celibacy. He contributed to the development of plain song, frequently called Gregorian Chant. Reference here is to his commentary on the Book of Job called *Morals on the Book of Job*, 3 vols. (Oxford: J. H. Parker, 1845), Bk. XXII, chap. 2, pp. 546–547.

[45] Aristotle, *Nicomachean Ethics* II. 6, 1106a15–19.

This, however, happens in two ways: formally and materially. It happens formally when some habit orders one to a good as good, and materially when one is ordered to something good, but not under the aspect of good.

The good, insofar as it is good, is the object of the appetitive part alone. For the good is what all desire.[46] Therefore, those habits which either are in the appetitive part, or depend upon the appetitive part, are ordered formally to the good. Hence, these in particular have the character *virtue*. Those habits which neither are in the appetitive part nor depend upon it can be ordered materially, but not formally—that is, under the aspect of good—to that which is good. Hence, they can in some way be called virtues, but not in the proper sense, like the previous habits.

It must be understood, however, that the speculative, as well as the practical, intellect is capable of being perfected by some habit in two ways. In one way the intellect can be perfected absolutely and of itself, insofar as it precedes the will and, as it were, moves it.[47] It can be perfected in another way, insofar as it follows the will, as it were, eliciting its action under the command of the will. As has been said,[48] both of these potencies, intellect and will, act in concert with each other.

Those habits, therefore, which are in the practical or speculative intellect according to the first way can in some sense be called virtues, although they are not so in the perfect sense. In this way understanding, science, and wisdom [49] are in

[46] Actually a quotation from Aristotle. See his *Nicomachean Ethics* I. 1, 1094a3. For an extensive treatment of goodness by Aquinas, see his *De Veritate*, q. 21, aa. 1-6.

[47] On the relation of intellect and will, see St. Thomas, *Summa Theologiae*, I–II, 9, 2c; *De Veritate*, q. 22, a. 12; *Summa Contra Gentiles*, III, 26; *De Malo*, q. 6.

[48] See above, pp. 86–88.

[49] St. Thomas is using Aristotle's list of the speculative intellect's virtues. See *Nicomachean Ethics* VI. 3–8, 1139b14–1142a31. See St. Thomas, *Summa Theologiae*, I, 79, 12c; I–II, 53, 1c; *Summa Contra Gentiles*, I, 94; II, 4; III, 37 and 43; IV, 12.

the speculative intellect, and art [50] is in the practical intellect. Moreover, someone is said to possess understanding or science to the extent that his intellect is perfected for knowing truth, which, indeed, is the good of the intellect. But although this truth can be willed, inasmuch as a man might will to understand a truth, nevertheless the aforementioned habits do not perfect the man to do this. For a man is not made desirous of considering truth through the habit of science, but only made capable of such consideration. Hence, the consideration itself of truth is not science inasmuch as this consideration is willed, but according as science tends directly to its object. The case is similar for art with respect to the practical intellect. Art does not perfect a man so that he wills to operate well according to that art, but only so that he knows how, and is able, to do something well.

Habits of the speculative or practical intellect, insofar as it follows the will, have the character virtue more truly because by them a man not only has the ability or know-how to act rightly, but he wills to act rightly. This is evident in both faith [51] and prudence,[52] but in different ways.

Faith perfects the speculative intellect according as it is commanded to believe by the will. This is evident from the act of faith. A man assents intellectually to those things which surpass human reason only because he wills to do so. As Augustine says,[53] man cannot believe unless he so wills. Faith will be in the speculative intellect according as it submits to the command of the will, as temperance is in the concupiscible appetite according as it submits to the command of reason. Hence, the will commands the intellect in believing, not only as to the execution of the act, but even as to the determina-

---

[50] On this notion of art, see St. Thomas, *Summa Theologiae*, I, 57, 3c and 4c; *Summa Contra Gentiles*, I, 93; II, 24.

[51] On St. Thomas' notion of faith, see his *Summa Theologiae*, II–II, 1, 1c; *De Veritate*, 14, 8c.

[52] On prudence, see St. Thomas, *Summa Theologiae*, II–II, 47, 1c and 2c; *Summa Contra Gentiles*, III, 35.

[53] Augustine, *In Iohannis Evangelium*, in *Corpus Christianorum* (Tourhout, Belgium: Brepols, 1954), tract XXVI, no. 2 (Vol. XXXVIII, p. 260).

tion of the object, inasmuch as the intellect assents through the command of the will to a determinate credible object, just as the concupiscible appetite tends through temperance to an object determined by reason as a mean.

Prudence, indeed, is in the practical intellect or reason, as has been said; [54] not, however, in such a way that the will determines the object of prudence. It determines only the end. Prudence, however, does inquire about the object. For, pre-supposing the good end from the will, prudence inquires about the ways through which this good can be procured and preserved.

Thus it is evident that the habits existing in the intellect are related to the will in diverse ways.

Some depend on the will only with regard to their use. This dependence is, indeed, accidental, since the use of habits of this kind depends in one way on the will and in another way on the aforementioned habits, such as science, wisdom, and art. For by these habits man is not perfected in such a way that he wills to use these habits well, but only in such a way that he is made capable of using them well.

One intellectual habit depends upon the will as upon that from which it receives its principle. For in operative things the end is the principle. This is the case with prudence.

Another of the habits depends on the will for the determination of its object as well. This is the case with faith. Although all these habits can in some way or another be called virtues, these last two more perfectly and properly have the character *virtue*. It does not follow from this, however, that they are the more noble or more perfect habits.

Article VIII

Whether Virtues Are in Us by Nature

REPLY: It must be said that just as there are different views on the production of natural forms, so there are dif-ferent views on the attainment of science and virtue.

[54] See two paragraphs above.

There were some who held that the forms pre-existed actually in matter but in a hidden fashion, and that they were brought from a hidden state to a manifest one by a natural agent. This was the opinion of Anaxagoras,[55] who held that all things were in all things in such a way that all things could be generated from all things.

Others, however, said that the source of the forms was totally extrinsic, either by participation in the ideas, as Plato held,[56] or from the agent intellect, as Avicenna claimed.[57] These contended that natural agents merely disposed matter for a form.

The third opinion is the middle one of Aristotle, which posits that the forms pre-exist potentially in matter and are reduced to act by an extrinsic natural agent.[58]

Similarly, with respect to the sciences and virtues, some claim that they are in us by nature, and that study only removes the impediments to science and virtue. This appears to be what Plato held, for he claimed that the sciences and virtues are caused in us by a participation in the separated forms, but the soul is impeded from using them through union with the body.[59] This impediment had to be removed

55 Anaxagoras (ca. 500–ca. 428 B.C.), a Greek philosopher, credited with bringing philosophy to Athens. His outstanding contribution to philosophy was his postulation of an all-pervading Mind (nous) which accounts for the order in the universe. St. Thomas' knowledge of the pre-Socratic philosophers was based largely upon Aristotle's accounts. Anaxagoras' view of generation is described by Aristotle in his Metaphysics I. 3, 984a12–16.

56 Plato (ca. 427–ca. 347 B.C.), the great Athenian philosopher, seems to have held (and certainly was so interpreted in the Middle Ages) that types of things, e.g., justice, goodness, horseness, were real and were separated from the things of this world, which were thought to be imitations of them. See Plato, Parmenides 132b ff., Timaeus 51c ff., Republic 476a ff., in Collected Dialogues of Plato, eds. E. Hamilton and H. Cairns (New York: Bollingen Foundation, 1961).

57 Avicenna, De Anima, Pt. V, chap. 5A.

58 Aristotle, On Generation and Corruption I. 3, 317b16–18; I. 9, 326b29–327a1; On the Generation of Animals II. 3, 736b10–12.

59 St. Thomas' knowledge of Plato was largely based on Aristotelian accounts. Aristotle quotes Plato frequently on this point, e.g., Prior Analytics II. 21, 67a22; Metaphysics I. 9, 991b3 and XIII. 5, 1080a2. Relevant passages from Plato are Meno 81c–86c and Phaedo 96a–100e.

through study of the sciences and the exercise of the virtues.

Others, indeed, said that the sciences and virtues are in us through the influence of the agent intellect, for the reception of whose influence man is disposed through study and practice. The third is the intermediate opinion: sciences and virtues are in us by nature according to aptitude, but their perfection is not in us by nature. This opinion is better because just as the virtue of natural agents takes away nothing with respect to natural forms, so study and practice maintain its efficacy with respect to the attainment of science and virtue.

It should be understood, however, that an aptitude for a perfection and a form can exist in a subject in two ways: in one way according to passive potency only, like the aptitude in the matter of air for the form of fire; in another way according to passive and active potency at once, like the aptitude in a diseased body for health, inasmuch as the body is receptive to health. It is in this latter fashion that man has a natural aptitude for virtue—partly because of the nature of his species, insofar as the aptitude for virtue is common to all men, and partly because of the makeup of an individual, insofar as certain men are more apt for virtue than others.

As evidence for this it must be known that there can be a threefold subject of virtue in man, as is evident above,[60] namely, the intellect, the will, and the inferior appetite, which is divided into the concupiscible and the irascible. In any one we must consider in some way both the susceptibility to virtue and the active principle of virtue.

It is clear that in the intellective part there is a possible intellect [61] which is in potency to all intelligibles, in the cognition of which consists intellectual virtue. There is also the agent intellect,[62] by whose light the intelligibles come to be in

---

48 See above: art. IV (pp. 81 ff.); art. V (pp. 84 ff.); art. VI (pp. 86 ff.); art. VII (pp. 88 ff.).

61 *Possible intellect:* the power of intellectual cognition, usually referred to simply as the intellect. Cf. above, *On Being and Essence,* notes 52 and 53 (pp. 51 and 52).

62 Cf. above, *On Being and Essence,* notes 52 and 53 (pp. 51 and 52).

act, some of which are from the beginning immediately and naturally known by man without study or inquiry. These are first principles,[63] not only in speculative matters, such as "every whole is greater than any one of its parts," and similar ones, but also in practical matters, such as "evil is to be avoided" and the like. Known naturally, these are the principles of all subsequent cognition acquired by study, be it practical or speculative.

Similarly, it is clear that the will is a certain natural, active principle, since it is naturally inclined to the ultimate end. The end, however, in practical matters has the character of a natural principle. Therefore, the inclination of the will is a certain active principle with respect to every disposition that is acquired through practice in the affective part.[64] Moreover, it is clear that the will itself, insofar as it is a potency undetermined to any means to an end, is susceptible of an habitual inclination to this one or that one.

The irascible and concupiscible appetites, however, are naturally subject to reason. Hence, they are naturally receptive to virtue, which is perfected in them according as they are disposed to follow the good of reason.

All the aforementioned beginnings of virtues are consequent upon the nature of the human species and, hence, are common to all men.

There is, however, a certain beginning of virtue which is consequent upon the nature of the individual, according as a man, from his natural makeup or from a celestial impression,[65] is inclined to the act of some virtue. This inclination is indeed a certain beginning of virtue. It is not, however,

[63] See above, note 49 (p. 89).

[64] *Affective part:* a term embracing will and the irascible and concupisciple powers. It is usually used in opposition to *cognitive part.* Cf. St. Thomas, *De Veritate,* q. X, a. 9 ad 7.

[65] St. Thomas refers here to some outmoded astronomical theories of Aristotle. Aristotle believed that heavenly bodies affect and change things on earth. See Aristotle, *On Generation and Corruption* II. 10, 336b16–20. Cf. Sir David Ross, *Aristotle* (London: Methuen and Co., 1960), pp. 95–99, 107–108; St. Thomas, *De Potentia,* q. 6, a. 3c.

perfect virtue, because perfect virtue requires the moderation of reason. Hence, the definition of virtue includes the choice of a means according to right reason. For if someone follows an inclination of this sort without the discretion of reason, he frequently sins. And just as the beginning of virtue without the operation of reason lacks the character of perfect virtue, so also do some of the things which precede virtue.

For one proceeds through the investigation of reason from universal principles to special cases. Through the function of reason, man is led from the desire for the ultimate end to those things which are conducive to that end. Reason itself in directing the irascible and concupiscible appetites makes them subject to itself. Accordingly it is evident that complete virtue requires the work of reason, whether the virtue be in the intellect, in the will, or in the concupiscible or the irascible appetite.

In summary, the beginning of virtue in the superior part is ordered to the virtue of the inferior part. Thus a man is prepared for virtue in his will by the beginning of virtue in his will and intellect. Man is prepared for virtue in the irascible and concupiscible appetites by the beginning of virtue in them, and by the beginning of virtue which is in the superior parts but not vice versa. Hence, it is also clear that reason, which is superior, operates for the completion of all virtue.

Moreover, the operative principle is divided in two: one is reason, as opposed to the other, which is nature, as is evident in the second book of the *Physics*.[66] Their difference lies in this: the rational power is ordered to opposites, while nature is ordered to one. Hence it is clear that the completion of virtue is not by nature but by reason.

[66] Aristotle, *Physics* II. 6, 198a11–12.

Article IX

Whether Virtues Are Acquired by Actions

REPLY: It must be said that since a virtue is the ultimate perfection of a potency to which any potency extends itself so that it operate, that is, so that the operation be good, it is clear that the virtue of anything is that through which it produces a good operation. Because everything exists for the sake of its operation [67] and, moreover, because everything is good insofar as it is properly related to its end,[68] each thing must be good and must operate well through a virtue proper to it.

Moreover, the proper good of one thing is not the same as the proper good of another, for there are diverse perfections corresponding to the diverse capacities for perfections. Accordingly man's good is other than a horse's or a rock's good. In addition, man's good is taken in various ways, according to the diverse viewpoints which can be adopted toward him. The good of man, as a man, is different from his good as a citizen.

The good of a man as man consists in the perfection of his reason in the cognition of truth and in the regulation of his inferior appetites according to the rule of reason, for a man is man by his rationality. However, the good of man as a citizen lies in his being ordered to the good of all within a commonwealth. Because of this the Philosopher says in Book Three of the *Politics* [69] that the virtue by which a man is a good man is not the same as the virtue by which a man is a good citizen. Man, however, is not only a terrestrial citizen

[67] On the notion of perfection through action, see St. Thomas, *Summa Theologiae*, I–II, 3, 2c; 32, 1c.

[68] On the relation of good and end, see St. Thomas, *Summa Contra Gentiles*, III, 3 and 24; *Summa Theologiae*, I, 5, 1c.

[69] Aristotle, *Politics* III. 4, 1276b35 and 1277a1,

but a participant in the heavenly city, Jerusalem,[70] whose governor is the Lord and whose citizens comprise the angels and all the saints, whether they reign in glory and are at peace in Heaven, or are travelers on earth. This accords with the words of the Apostle in Ephesians 2:19: "You are citizens with the saints and members of God's family," etc. To be a participant in this city, man's nature does not suffice. It must be elevated to this by the grace of God.[71] For it is evident that those virtues which are in man as a participant in this city cannot be acquired by him by his own natural powers. Hence, they are not caused by our actions, but are infused in us by divine favor.

The virtues, however, which are in a man as man, or in him as a citizen of an earthly commonwealth, do not exceed the faculty of human nature. Hence, man can acquire them by actions proper to him through his natural powers. This is evident by what follows.

Anything with the natural aptitude for some perfection can acquire it. But if this aptitude arises from a passive principle alone, then it cannot be acquired by an action proper to the thing, but only by the action of some natural exterior agent, just as the air receives light from the sun. If, however, something has the natural aptitude for a certain perfection arising out of a principle that is active and passive at once, then it can acquire the perfection through an action proper to itself, as the body of a sick man which has a natural aptitude for health. And because a subject is naturally receptive of health through a natural, active virtue oriented to healing, it follows that a sick man is sometimes cured without the action of an exterior agent.

It was shown, however, in the preceding question that the natural aptitude for virtue that man possesses arises out of principles which are both active and passive. The very order

70 Jerusalem, often under the name Zion, figures familiarly in both Jewish and Christian literature as a symbol for the capital of the Messiah and the prototype of the heavenly city.

71 On grace, see St. Thomas, *De Veritate*, XXVII, aa. 1–7; *Summa Theologiae*, I–II, 110, 1c; *Summa Contra Gentiles*, III, 150.

of potencies makes this clear. In the intellective part there is a quasi-passive principle, the possible intellect, which is reduced to its perfection by the agent intellect. The intellect in act, moreover, moves [72] the will, since the known good is the end which moves an appetite. The will, however, moved by reason, is meant to move the sensitive appetite,[73] namely, the irascible and concupiscible powers, which in turn are meant to obey reason. Accordingly, it is also evident that any virtue which makes a human operation good has a proper act in man, who, by his action, can reduce the virtue to act, be it in the intellect, the will, or the irascible or concupiscible appetite.

Virtues in the intellective part and in the appetitive part, however, are actualized in different ways. The action of the intellect and of the cognitive virtue of the intellect consists in its assimilation [74] of the knowable object in a certain way. Hence, intellectual virtue comes about in the intellective part by means of the intellectual species [75] being made present in it, either actually or habitually, by the agent intellect. The action of the appetitive virtue, however, consists in a certain inclination to the appetible object. Hence, in order for virtue to come about in the appetitive part an inclination to some determinate thing must be given to it.

It should be known, moreover, that the inclination of natural things follows their form and is therefore an inclination to one through the exigency of the form. As long as this form remains, such inclination cannot be taken away nor can the contrary inclination be induced. Because of this, natural things do not become accustomed or unaccustomed to something. For however often a rock is raised, it never becomes accustomed to this raised position, but always is inclined to

---

72 See above, note 47 (p. 89).

73 On the will's relation to inferior powers, see St. Thomas, *Summa Theologiae*, I, 81, 3c; I–II, 17, 7c; *De Veritate*, q. 25, a. 4.

74 In order to know, the knower must possess in a cognitive way the object known. See St. Thomas, *In De An.*, Bk. II, lect. 12, no. 377.

75 The species of the intellect is produced by the agent intellect using the phantasm. See above, notes 61 and 62. See also St. Thomas, *Quodlibet*, VIII, q. 2, a. 1.

descend. Those things, however, which are related to both do not have a form through which they are turned aside to one determinately. Rather, they are determined to some one by the proper mover. By being determined to it, they are disposed in a certain way to the same thing. Since they are inclined on many different occasions, they are determined to the same thing by the proper mover, and the determinate inclination to that thing grows firm. This superadded disposition is something like a form which tends in the way nature does to one thing. It is on account of this that custom is said to be another nature.

Therefore, since the appetitive power is related to a number of objects, it does not tend to one of them unless it is determined to it by reason. Therefore, when reason repeatedly inclines the appetitive power to some one object, a certain firm disposition becomes established in the appetitive power, through which it is inclined to the one thing to which it is accustomed. This disposition thus established is a habit of virtue.

Therefore, if it be rightly considered, a virtue of the appetitive part is nothing other than a certain disposition or form marked and impressed upon the appetitive power by reason. Because of this, however strong the disposition to something be in the appetitive power, it cannot have the character of virtue unless reason is involved. Accordingly, reason is put in the definition of virtue, for the Philosopher states in Book Two of the *Ethics* [76] that virtue is a chosen habit in the mind consisting of a determinate species insofar as a man of wisdom will determine it.

Article X

Whether Any Virtues Are in Man by Infusion

REPLY: It must be said that in addition to the virtues acquired by our own actions, as have already been discussed,[77]

[76] Aristotle, *Nicomachean Ethics* II. 6, 1107a1–3.
[77] See art. IX, above (pp. 96 ff.).

one must posit other virtues that are infused in man by God.

The reason for this can be understood from the fact that virtue, as the Philosopher says in Book Two of the *Ethics*,[78] is what makes its possessor good and renders his operation good. Therefore, in accordance with the various ways in which good is found in man, there must also be a diversification of virtues. This is evident from the fact that some things are good for a man insofar as he is man, while others are good for him as citizen. It is manifest that some operations can be appropriate for a man as man which, however, are not appropriate for him as citizen. On account of this, the Philosopher states in the third book of the *Politics*[79] that one virtue makes a man be a good man, whereas another makes him be a good citizen.

In addition, we must consider that man's good is twofold: one good is proportioned to his nature, and another exceeds the faculty of his nature.

The reason for this is that whatever is passive must follow in different ways perfections coming from an agent, according to the agent's diversity of power. Thus we note that the perfections and forms which are caused by the action of a natural agent do not exceed the natural faculty of the recipient. For a natural, active power is proportioned to a natural, passive potency.[80] But perfections and forms which arise from a supernatural agent of infinite power, which God is, exceed the faculty of the nature that receives them. Accordingly the rational soul, which is caused immediately by God, so exceeds the capacity of its matter that corporeal matter is not totally capable of grasping and confining it.[81] Some power and operation of it remains in which corporeal matter does not com-

---

[78] Aristotle, *Nicomachean Ethics* II. 6, 1106a15–19.

[79] Aristotle, *Politics* III. 4, 1276b35 and 1277a1.

[80] On this relationship, see St. Thomas, *Summa Theologiae*, I, 25, 1c and 3c; *De An.*, q. *unica*, a. 12.

[81] For St. Thomas' view of the human soul, see his *De An.*, q. *unica*, a. 1; *Summa Theologiae*, I, 75, 2c; 76, 1c; *Summa Contra Gentiles*, II, 56–59. Cf. Gilson, *The Christian Philosophy of St. Thomas Aquinas* (New York: Random House, 1956), pp. 187–199.

municate. This occurs with none of the other forms, which are caused by natural agents.

So, just as man acquires his first perfection, namely, the soul, from the action of God,[82] so also does he immediately receive from God his ultimate perfection, which is the perfect happiness of man. In this he is at rest. This is evident from the fact that man's natural desire can in no other way be satisfied except in God alone. For man has an innate desire whereby from effects he is moved to seek causes. Nor is this desire satisfied until man has arrived at the first cause, which is God.[83]

It is necessary, therefore, that just as the first perfection of man, the rational soul, exceeds the faculty of corporeal matter, so the ultimate perfection which man can reach, the beatitude of eternal life, exceeds the faculty of the whole of human nature. And because everything is ordered to an end through some operation, and also because the means to the end must in some way be proportioned to that end, man must possess some perfections by which he is ordered to a supernatural end, which perfections exceed the faculty of his natural principles. This could not be unless God infused into man certain supernatural principles of operation in addition to his natural principles.

The natural principles of operation are the essence of the soul and its powers, namely, the intellect and the will. These are the principles of operations of man as man. Nor could this be so unless the intellect had a knowledge of principles through which it is directed to the cognition of other things, and unless the will had a natural inclination to the good of nature proportioned to it, as was stated in the preceding question.

---

[82] On the creation of the human soul, see St. Thomas, *Summa Theologiae*, I, 90, 2c and 3c; *Summa Contra Gentiles*, II, 86 and 87; *De Potentia*, q. 3, a. 9; *Quodlibet*, IX, q. 5, a. 1.

[83] The union with God is by way of knowledge and love. See St. Thomas, *Summa Theologiae*, I–II, 3, 8; *De Veritate*, q. 8, a. 1; *Quodlibet*, IX, q. 8, a. unica.

Therefore, in order for man to carry on those actions which are ordered to the end of eternal life, there is divinely infused in man first and foremost grace, through which his soul has a certain spiritual existence. In addition, faith, hope, and charity are infused.[84] Through faith, the intellect is enlightened to know certain supernatural things, which in this order behave as the naturally known principles in the order of connatural[85] operations. Through hope and charity, the will acquires a certain inclination to that supernatural good to which the human will is not sufficiently ordered through its natural inclination.

Thus just as, in addition to the natural principles, habits of virtue are required for the perfection of man in the order connatural to him, as has been said above,[86] so also, by way of divine influence, man acquires in addition to the previously mentioned supernatural principles certain infused virtues by which he is perfected for ordering his operations to the end of eternal life.

Article XI

Whether Infused Virtue Is Increased

REPLY: It must be said that many are in error concerning forms, as a result of their judging them in the way in which they judge substances. This seems to occur because in the abstract forms are signified as substances are, like whiteness and virtue and the like. Hence, some following this way of speaking judge forms as if they were substances.

From this arises the error both of those who hold that the forms are hidden, and of those who hold that the forms were

[84] On these virtues and their necessity, see St. Thomas, *Summa Theologiae*, I–II, 62, 1c.

[85] *Connatural:* a term referring to inclinations or operations in accordance with a nature, e.g., understanding is connatural for man. The knowledge of supernatural matters is therefore connatural for a man in grace.

[86] See above, arts. I and II (pp. 75–79).

in existence from creation. They hold that forms are capable of change just as substances are.[87] Wherefore, not finding that whence forms are generated, they posit them either as created or as pre-existing in matter. They do not see that just as the act of existing is not united to the form, but to the subject through the form,[88] so, too, change, which terminates in existence, does not belong to the form but to the subject. For just as the form is called a being, not because it exists, properly speaking, but because by it something exists, so too the form is said to change, not because it itself changes, but because by it something comes to be; as when, for example, a subject is reduced from potency to act.

Accordingly, in discussions concerning the intensification of qualities, some speak as if the qualities and forms were substances. A substance is said to grow insofar as it is the subject of change through which it moves from a lesser quantity to a greater one. This is called the change of augmentation. And because the growth of a substance occurs through the addition of one substance to another, certain men held that it is in this way that charity, or any infused virtue, is increased—that is, by the addition of charity to charity, or of virtue to virtue, or of whiteness to whiteness. This is entirely impossible, for the addition of one to another cannot be understood unless duality was previously known. But duality in forms of one species cannot be understood except through the otherness of the subject, for the forms of one species are not numerically distinct except through the subject.[89] If, therefore, quality is added to quality, one of the following must occur: either subject is added to subject—for example, one white thing is added to another white thing—or else something in the subject becomes white which previously was

[87] Reference is to Augustine. See his *De Genesi ad Litteram*, Bk. VI, pt. 6, in *Corpus Scriptorum Ecclesiasticorum Latinorum*, Vol. XXVIII, pt. 2, pp. 176–178.

[88] See above, *The Principles of Nature*, note 5 (p. 8).

[89] See above, *On Being and Essence*, chap. II and note 25 (p. 38); chap. V (pp. 58–62).

not white, as certain people held concerning corporeal qualities. The Philosopher disproves this, however, in Book Four
of the *Physics*.[90] For when something becomes more curved,
something does not become curved which was previously not
curved. Rather, the whole thing becomes more curved. It is
impossible to suppose this in regard to spiritual qualities
whose subject is the soul, or part of the soul.

Wherefore certain other men contended that charity and
the other infused virtues do not grow essentially. Rather,
they said growth meant either that the virtues are more deeply
rooted in the subject, or that they operate with more fervor
or intensity. This position would indeed have some merit, if
charity were a certain substance having an act of existing
apart from substance. Hence, the author of the *Sentences*,[91]
thinking charity to be a certain substance, namely, the Holy
Spirit Himself, seems, not unreasonably, to have held this
type of increase. But others, holding that charity is a certain
quality, thus have spoken in an utterly irrational way.

For some quality to increase is nothing more than for the
subject to participate more in the quality, since a quality
cannot exist except in a subject. From its greater participation
in the quality, the subject acts more vehemently, inasmuch as
anything acts insofar as it is in act.[92] Hence, what is reduced
more fully to act, acts more perfectly. Therefore, to hold
that a certain quality is not increased essentially but is increased by a deeper rooting in the subject or according to
the intensity of its act is to posit contradictories to be the
case simultaneously.

---

90 Aristotle, *Physics* IV. 9, 217a20–217b10.

91 Peter Lombard (*ca.* 1100–*ca.* 1160), an Italian theologian, who contributed extensively to the development of theological speculation by
composing his *Sentences,* a compilation of varying theological opinions
by many authors on practically all theological topics. The *Sentences*
became for later medieval theologians a matter for comment and
discussion.

92 On the relation between existing and acting, see St. Thomas,
Summa Theologiae, I, 76, 1c; 104, 1c; *Summa Contra Gentiles,* I, 73; II,
47, 52, 81.

Therefore, there remains for us to consider how certain qualities and forms are said to be increased, and what those things are which can be increased.

It should be understood that since names are signs of things understood, as is said in the first book of *On Interpretation*,[93] and just as from the things better known we know those things which are less fully known, so from those things better known we name those things which are less fully known. Hence, because local motion is the best known of all motions, from contrariety according to place the name "distance" is derived and applied to all contraries between which there can be some change, as the Philosopher says in the tenth book of the *Metaphysics*.[94] Similarly, because quantitative change in substances is more easily sensed than alteration, the names which are suitable to quantitative change are applied to alteration. Hence, just as a body moved to a perfect quantity is said to be increased, and the perfect quantity itself is said to be great with respect to the imperfect, so also what is moved from an imperfect quality to a perfect one is said to be increased qualitatively, and the perfect quality itself is called great with respect to the imperfect. Because the perfection of anything is its goodness, therefore Augustine says that in those things which are not large in size, being larger is the same as being better.

To be changed from an imperfect form to a perfect one is nothing more than for a subject to be reduced more fully to act. For a form is act. Hence, for the subject to possess more fully the form is nothing more than for the subject to be reduced more fully to the act of that form. Just as something is reduced by an agent from pure potency to the act of a form, so also something is reduced by the action of an agent from imperfect act to perfect act.

This, however, does not happen in all forms, for two reasons.

The first flows from the very nature of the form, that is, that what perfects the nature *form* is something indivisible;

93 Aristotle, *On Interpretation* 1, 16a4.
94 Aristotle, *Metaphysics* X. 4, 10055a4–9.

as an example of this consider any number. An added unity constitutes a species. Hence, twoness or threeness is not said according to more or less. Consequently more or less is not found in quantities which are denominated by numbers, like bicubit or tricubit; [95] nor in figures, like three-sided or four-sided; nor in proportions, like double or triple.

The other reason stems from the relationship of the form to the subject, for it inheres in the subject in an indivisible way. For this reason a substantial form neither increases nor decreases insofar as it accounts for the substantial act of existing, which can only be in one manner; that is, where there is another substantial act of existing there is another thing. Because of this the Philosopher, in Book Eight of the *Metaphysics*,[96] likens definitions to numbers. Hence nothing which is substantially predicated of another, even if it be in the genus *accident*, is predicated according to more and less. For whiteness is not called more or less a color. Because of this, qualities signified abstractly, inasmuch as they are signified after the manner of substance are neither increased nor decreased. For whiteness is not called more or less, but the white thing is.

Neither of these two apply to charity and the other infused virtues as reasons for their not being increased or decreased. This is so because their nature is not something indivisible, like the nature of number, nor do they account for any substantial act of existing, like substantial forms. They are, therefore, increased or decreased as their subject is reduced more fully to their act through the action of the agent causing them. Hence, just as acquired virtues are increased by the actions through which they are caused, so infused virtues are increased by the action of God Who causes them.

Our actions are related to the growth of charity and the infused virtues as dispositions for receiving charity from the

[95] A cubit was an ancient unit of measurement, equal in length to the distance from the elbow to the tip of the middle finger of an adult's arm. A bicubit was double, and a tricubit triple, that distance.

[96] Aristotle, *Metaphysics* VIII. 3, 1043b34.

beginning. For a man doing what he can prepares himself to receive charity from God. Our later acts can be meritorious with respect to the growth of charity because they presuppose charity, which is the principle of merit.[97] But no one can merit without obtaining charity from the beginning, because merit cannot exist without charity. Therefore we say that charity grows in intensity.

Article XII

Whether There Is a Difference Among the Virtues

REPLY: It must be said that anything is specifically distinct according to that which is formal in it.[98] Moreover, that is formal in anything which completes its definition. For the ultimate difference constitutes the species. Hence, through the ultimate difference, one defined thing differs specifically from others. Moreover, if the difference is formally multipliable through diverse characteristics, the defined thing is divided into different species according to that diversity.

That which completes and is ultimately formal in the definition of virtue is the good. For virtue is universally understood to be defined as "what makes its possessor good and renders his action good," as is evident from Book Two of the *Ethics*.[99] Accordingly, human virtue, of which we are speaking, must be specifically diversified according to the formal diversification of the good.

Since man, moreover, is man insofar as he is rational, the good of man must be the good of that which is in some way rational. Now the rational or intellective part embraces both the cognitive and the appetitive elements. Moreover, not only does the will, which follows the apprehension of

[97] On merit, see St. Thomas, *Summa Theologiae*, I–II, 21, 3 and 4; q. 114, a. 4.
[98] On the substantial form, see above, *On Being and Essence*, chap. III, *passim* (pp. 48–50).
[99] Aristotle, *Nicomachean Ethics* II, 6, 1106a15–19.

the intellect, pertain to the rational part, but so also does the sensitive appetite, divided into the irascible and the concupiscible. For in man this appetite too follows the apprehension of reason, insofar as it obeys the command of reason. Hence, it is said also to participate in some way in reason. Therefore, the good of the cognitive and of the appetitive part constitutes the good of man.

However, the good is not attributed to each part for the same reason. For the good is attributed formally to the appetitive part, inasmuch as the good itself is the object of the appetitive part. Good is not attributed formally, but only materially, to the intellective part.[100] For to know the truth is a certain good of the cognitive part, although it is not related to the cognitive part as a good, but rather to the appetitive part. For knowledge of truth is something desirable.

It is, therefore, necessary that the virtues which perfect the cognitive part for knowing the truth, and the virtue which perfects the rational appetite for apprehending the good, be of different kinds. On account of this, the Philosopher in his *Ethics*[101] distinguishes the intellectual from the moral virtues. Those are called intellectual which perfect the intellectual part for the cognition of truth, while those are called moral which perfect the appetitive part for seeking the good.

Because the good is much more appropriate to the appetitive than to the intellective part, the name "virtue" is more suitably and properly applied to the virtues of the appetitive part than to those of the intellective part, although the intellectual virtues are nobler perfections than the moral virtues, as is proved in Book Six of the *Ethics*.[102]

Moreover, the knowledge of truth is not of one kind with respect to all things. The knowledge of necessary truth is

---

[100] On the object of the intellect, see St. Thomas, *Summa Theologiae*, I, 5, 2c; 58, 4c; *Summa Contra Gentiles*, II, 98.

[101] Aristotle, *Nicomachean Ethics* I. 13, 1103a4–6.

[102] *Ibid.*, VI. 13, 1145a6–11.

different from the knowledge of contingent truth. Moreover, necessary truth is known in one way if it is known in and by itself, like the knowledge of first principles, whereas it is known in another way if the knowledge comes about through another, like the knowledge of conclusions through science or wisdom, which concerns itself with the highest things. The knowledge of the latter is still another kind of knowing, in that through it man is directed to knowing other things.

The same can be said regarding contingent products. The knowledge of what we can do [agibilia] interiorly, like our operations, concerning which we frequently err because of some passion and with which prudence is concerned, is not the same kind as the knowledge of those things outside of us which we can make [factibilia] and which are directed by some art. The passions of the soul, moreover, do not interfere with the correct estimation of the latter.

Accordingly, in Book Six of the Ethics,[103] the Philosopher lists the intellectual virtues as wisdom, science, understanding, prudence, and art.

Similarly the good of the appetitive part is not the same kind in all human affairs. This kind of good can be investigated in three different areas: the passions of the irascible appetite, the passions of the concupiscible appetite, and our operations that deal with the exterior things we use, like buying and selling, hiring, entering into contracts, and other such things.

The good for man as far as his passions are concerned lies in his so possessing them that through their impetus he is not diverted from the judgment of reason. Accordingly, if there are certain passions which are apt to impede the good of reason by way of exciting a man to act or to seek something, the good of virtue consists especially in a certain restraint and hesitation. This is evident in temperance, which restrains and curbs our desires. If, however, a passion is apt severely to interfere with the good of reason by way of

103 Aristotle, Nicomachean Ethics VI. 2, 1139b15–18.

restraint, such as fear, the good of virtue concerning a passion of this kind will lie in maintaining action. This is accomplished by fortitude.

Concerning exterior things, the good of reason consists in their receiving due proportion according as they pertain to the goods proper to human living. The name of justice is imposed from this, for the function of justice is to direct and to find equality in things of this sort.[104]

We must note, however, that the good of both the intellective part and the appetitive part is twofold: namely, the good that is the ultimate end, and the good that is the means to that end. Each has a different character. Therefore, in addition to all the aforementioned virtues according to which man pursues the good among means to the end, there must be other virtues whereby man rightly relates himself to his ultimate end, which is God. These virtues are called theological, because they have God not only as their end, but as their object.[105]

Moreover, in order for us to be moved rightly to the end, that end must be known and desired. Desire for the end requires two things: a confidence in obtaining the end, inasmuch as no wise man is moved to what cannot be attained; and a love of the end, inasmuch as nothing is desired unless it is loved. Therefore, there are three theological virtues, namely: faith, by which we know God; hope, by which we trust that we will attain Him; and charity, by which we love Him. In this way it is evident that there are three genera of virtues—theological, intellectual, and moral—and that each genus has many species under it.

---

[104] On this notion of equality, see St. Thomas, *Summa Theologiae,* II–II, 57, 1; 58, 1–3.

[105] On these virtues, see St. Thomas, *Summa Theologiae,* II–II, 1, 1c; 17, 1c; 23, 1c.

Article XIII

Whether Virtue Lies in a Mean

REPLY: It must be said that both the intellectual and the moral virtues lie in a mean,[106] although in different ways. The theological virtues, however, do not lie in a mean, except perhaps accidentally.

As evidence for this it should be recognized that the good of anything having a rule and measure consists in its being conformed to that rule or measure. Hence, we say that is good which has neither more nor less than it ought to have.

Moreover, it should be considered that the matter of the moral virtues is the passions and human operations, just as things which can be made [*factibilia*] are the matter of art. Therefore, just as the good in those things produced by art consists in the artifacts receiving a measure dictated by the art, which is the rule of artifacts, so the good in passions and human operations lies in the attainment of reason's measure, which is the measure and rule of all the passions and human operations. Since man is man because he has reason, his good must be in accordance with reason.

Moreover, evil in the passions or in human operations lies in someone exceeding the measure of reason, or falling short of it. Therefore since the good of man is human virtue, it follows that moral virtue consists in a mean between excess and defect—excess, defect, and mean being understood in relationship to the rule of reason.

As regards the intellectual virtues, which are in reason itself, certain ones are practical, like prudence and art, whereas others are speculative, like wisdom, science, and understanding. The matter of the practical virtues is the passions and human operations, or the artifacts themselves. The matter, however,

---

106 *Mean:* between the extremes of excess and defect. Cf. Aristotle, *Nicomachean Ethics* II. 5–7, 1105b19–1108b10; see St. Thomas, *Summa Theologiae*, I–II, q. 64, aa. 1–4.

of the speculative virtues is necessary things. Reason is related to each in a different way.

To those things that reason directs, reason is related as a rule or measure, as has already been stated.[107] To those things that it contemplates, reason is related as something that is measured or ruled is related to a rule and measure. For the good of our intellect is truth, which follows our intellect when it is conformed to a thing.[108]

Therefore, just as the moral virtues consist in a mean determined by reason, so it is the task of prudence, which is the virtue of the practical intellect concerned with moral matters, to impose that mean upon actions and passions. This is evident through the definition of moral virtue stated in Book Two of the *Ethics*: [109] an elective habit consisting in moderation, as determined by the wise man. Therefore, prudence and moral virtue have the same mean, but prudence is that which imposes it, while moral virtue is that upon which it is imposed, just as art and artifact have the same rectitude, the former as imposing it, the latter as receiving it.

Therefore, among the virtues of the speculative intellect the mean will be truth itself, which is considered in it insofar as it attains its measure. This, however, is not a mean between some extremes on the side of the thing known. Extremes between which the mean of virtue is understood are not peculiar to the measure, but to the measured, insofar as it exceeds or falls short of the measure. This is evident from what was said concerning the moral virtues. It is necessary, therefore, that the extremes between which lies the mean of intellectual virtues be understood as peculiar to the intellect itself.

The extremes of the intellect are opposed as affirmation and negation, as is evident in Book Two of *On Interpre-*

107 See two paragraphs above.

108 For a complete treatment of this very complicated problem, see St. Thomas, *De Veritate*, q. 1, aa. 1–12.

109 Aristotle, *Nicomachean Ethics* II. 6, 1107a1–3.

tation.[110] Between opposed affirmations and negations, therefore, lies the mean of the virtues of speculative intellect, which is the truth. Now the truth exists when what is, is said to be, and when what is not, is said not to be. Falsity will consist in an excess, when what is not is said to be; or in a defect, when what is, is said not to be.

Therefore, if there are no proper extremes in the intellect besides the extremes of things, then no mean or extremes are possible in the intellectual virtues. It is clear, moreover, that no extremes are proper to the will, except according to contrary things willed. This is so because the intellect knows something according as it is in the intellect, whereas the will is moved to something according as it is in itself. Hence, if there is any virtue in the will according to a relationship to its measure and rule, such virtue will not consist in a mean, for there cannot be extremes on the part of the measure but only on the part of the measured, insofar as it exceeds or falls short of the measure.

The theological virtues, however, are ordered to their matter or object, which is God, through the will. What is clear as regards charity and hope is maintained with respect to faith also. For, although faith is in the intellect, it is nevertheless in it as commanded by the will. For no one believes unless he wills to do so. Hence, since God is the rule and measure of the human will, it is clear that the theological virtues do not, strictly speaking, consist in a mean, although it might sometimes happen that certain of them consist in a mean accidentally, as will be explained later.[111]

---

[110] Aristotle, *On Interpretation* 1, 16a10–18.

[111] This disputation on the virtues was just one grouping among others which St. Thomas carried on during his teaching career. The reference to later treatment appears to indicate his plans for a future consideration of the topic. For the chronology of the disputations, see Gilson, *The Christian Philosophy of St. Thomas Aquinas*, pp. 389–391.

On Free Choice

Introduction to
On Free Choice

Freedom is a continual problem for mankind. When academicians discuss freedom, however, the various kinds of freedom are very frequently confused. One can talk about legal freedom, political freedom, academic freedom, freedom of speech, or even free enterprise—although St. Thomas' discussion of freedom, especially in this treatise, concerns none of these topics—but no matter what kind of freedom one is referring to, it always seems to be a property of something. One speaks of the press as free, speech as free, a professor in a classroom or laboratory as free, a person over twenty-one as free to enter into contracts. Note also that the property of freedom is predicated of a person or persons insofar as they are doing something—publishing, speaking, entering into contracts. Specifically, it is their actions which are free or nonfree.

To establish what St. Thomas means by the term "free choice" requires a very important distinction. The reader will recall from the treatise *On the Virtues* that Aquinas maintains that the nature of man is that of a composite of soul and body. This composite, a substance, possesses a number of powers—including the intellect, the will, the irascible appetite, and the concupiscible appetite—which are immediate sources of action. It is for this reason, in fact, that St. Thomas conceives powers as active potencies, or potencies for action. The actions of these powers, moreover, are immanent actions, that is, actions which commence and terminate in man, or do not affect anything external to him. Immanent actions, therefore, are different from transient actions. The act of enjoying the sight of a sunset is immanent. The act of commenting about it to a nearby friend is transient. The act of wanting a glass of water is immanent; the act of pouring it is transient. The act of being concerned about politics is immanent; the act of expressing one's concern by voting is transient.

When St. Thomas speaks of free choice he is speaking of an immanent act which is free. Hence free choice, as such, is not a matter of political or economic freedom, since these involve transient actions. Choice is an interior act. Our choices do indeed overflow into transient acts, but the two are distinct. Accordingly I might choose (immanent) milk instead of water, but this act is distinct from the act of reaching into the refrigerator for the milk bottle (transient). The problem of free choice is a problem of immanent actions.

In addition to the distinction between immanent and transient actions, St. Thomas' discussion of free choice demands a distinction between what have come to be called elicited and commanded acts of the will. The former are those acts which flow directly and immediately from the will, like choosing, desiring, or hating. Commanded acts of the will are those acts for which the will is responsible, but which flow from some power other than the will. For example, my will may be responsible for my walking, in the sense that I chose to walk, but walking is not an action performed by the will; through man's will, he may be responsible for his act of daydreaming, yet daydreaming is an act of his imagination.

Narrowing down the object of study in this treatise, then, one finds that freedom is a property of an action, an immanent action, specifically an elicited act of the will.

The reader may feel that by now he is aware of enough distinctions to confront the problem of free choice; but further clarifications are necessary. St. Thomas contends that the will is capable of a variety of actions, only one of which can be called choice. The act, for example, of commanding the imagination to daydream is not a choice. A choice may very well have preceded this command, but the latter, as such, is not the former.

It is possible now to determine with some precision the nature of an act of choice as conceived by St. Thomas. He maintains, first of all, that the will is a rational power or tendency, and accordingly he frequently calls it the rational appetite. The action of an appetite is difficult to describe except, perhaps, as an inner tendency. Negatively it can be said that its act is *not* one of being aware; yet its action is one that is dependent upon knowledge. The will cannot love or hate unless it is confronted by an object which is known as good, or bad, or harmful. The best word to describe all its actions is "tendency." Hence the will tends by loving, hating, and the like.

The will is a rational appetite. "Rational" here means that the acts of the will are dependent upon the knowledge produced by the intellect. To love justice or hate injustice are acts of the will responding (tending toward or away from) to things conceived by the intellect. The voluntary response, moreover, is to an object known intellectually as good or bad. The whole complicated question of which things are really good or bad, and whether individual preferences have any role to play in our judgments, is irrelevant here. Whatever one's predilections, Aquinas maintains one tends to them because one conceives them as good, or shuns them because one conceives them as bad or evil. Aquinas is saying that acts of the will ultimately depend upon acts of the intellect in what is technically called the order of finality—that is, the intellect must present an object as good or bad before an act of the will can come into being.

As we have seen above, the will can command other powers. The ability, according to St. Thomas, extends to the intellect. To show this, and finally get to the nature of choice, let us assume that the intellect presents some object to the will simply as being good, for example, a college education. The will responds to this object by what St. Thomas calls complacency, or love, or enjoyment. The high-school student then realizes that he is not in possession of this known good. The intellect, under the impetus of the aroused will, begins to enumerate the various means by which this good or end is attainable—money from parents, scholarships, or perhaps even theft. The rational election of one of these means is an act of choice.

A number of comments should be made here. First, the act of choice is concerned only with means to an end. An act of the will that takes pleasure in a good known only as an end is not an act of choice. Nor is a command to another power a choice. Choice is a selection of means to a known end. It does not matter, incidentally, whether or not the intellect has discovered one or more means to the end. The selection of one among many, or the act of accepting or refusing to take a unique means, or any of a group—each of these is understood as an act of choice.

Second, choice must involve the intellect. The act of choice is sometimes referred to as a composite act of intellect and will. Insofar as choice is a rational adherence to a means, it is possible to understand it in this fashion. In this treatise St. Thomas does insist that since choice denotes primarily movement or tendency, choice is primarily of the will. However, he never divorced the will's action from that of the intellect, since the will is totally dependent for its object upon the intellect. Choice, then, can best be understood as an act to which two powers contribute.

One final comment. Throughout this introduction choice is referred to as an action. Furthermore, not once has the term "free will" been used. This is in accord with Aquinas' terminology. Strictly speaking, only actions—specifically, choices —are free. St. Thomas does mention that inasmuch as choice arises primarily from the will, by extension the term can be predicated of the will. Hence, it is possible within Thomistic thought to speak of free will, but this would be a wide usage of the term "free."

This treatise *On Free Choice* is actually one question drawn from the larger work called the *De Veritate,* or *On Truth.* The latter is a disputation, and *On Free Choice* is its twenty-fourth question. As in *On the Virtues,* I have chosen to omit the objections and answers to objections of each article, for clarity's sake. The text is the twenty-fourth question of *De Veritate,* contained in the Marietti manual series, published in Turin.

On Free Choice

Article I

Whether Man Possesses Free Choice

REPLY: Without doubt it must be said that man has free choice. Faith demands that we hold this position, since without free choice one could not merit or demerit, or be justly rewarded or punished. There are clear indications of this if one considers the occasions when man appears to choose one thing freely and reject another. Finally, reason, too, demands that we hold this position, and following its dictates we examine the origin of free choice, proceeding in the following manner.[1]

In things that are moved or that move another, there is found this difference: some have within themselves the principle of their motion or operation, whereas others, such as things which are moved by violence have it outside themselves. In these, "the principle of motion is extrinsic to them, so that in receiving the force they contribute nothing," as the Philosopher states in the third book of the *Ethics*.[2] We cannot posit free choice in these, since they are not the cause of their motion. But that is free "which is its own cause," according to the Philosopher in the beginning of his *Metaphysics*.[3]

[1] It should be noted that St. Thomas' approach to the question of free choice is not the usual introspective one, wherein one notes the occasions when it is apparent that a man selects one alternative rather than another. In this paragraph he does mention such occasions, but his procedure is to analyze the genesis of internal movement, especially that of men, from which he develops his theory of freedom. Technically such an argument is a *propter quid* demonstration, or a demonstration by cause.

[2] Aristotle, *Nicomachean Ethics* III. 1, 110a1–4.

[3] Aristotle, *Metaphysics* I. 2, 982b26–28.

Among those whose principle of motion and operation is within themselves, some, such as animals, move themselves. Others, such as heavy and light things, do not move themselves even though they do have a certain interior principle of their motion. They do not move themselves since they cannot be distinguished into two parts, one of which would be the mover, the other the moved, as is found in animals. Although their movement follows a principle intrinsic to them, namely, the form, yet since they receive this form from that which generated them, they are said to be moved essentially by that which generated them, according to the Philosopher in the seventh book of the *Physics*.[4] They are said to be moved accidentally, however, by what removes the impediment to their motion. They are moved in themselves, but not by themselves. Hence, they do not possess free choice, since they themselves cause neither their motion nor their action. Rather, they are bound to acting and moving through what they receive from another.

Among those things which are moved by themselves, the motion of some proceeds from a judgment of reason, whereas the motion of others proceeds from a natural judgment.

Men act and are moved by a judgment of reason, for they deliberate about courses of action. All brute animals, however, act and are moved by a natural judgment. This is evident when you consider that all the members of a species act in a similar way, as, for example, swallows all build their nests in the same way. It is also evident from the fact that their judgment is determined to one course of action and not open to all, as bees are skilled in producing nothing but honeycombs. The case is similar for other animals.

Hence, it is clear to anyone who considers the matter rightly that the way in which motion and action are attributed to inanimate things of nature is the same as the way in which the judging of actions is attributed to brute animals. Just as heavy and light things do not move themselves such that they would be the causes of their own motion, so too

4 Aristotle, *Physics* VIII. 4, 255b24–256a3.

brutes do not judge of their own judgments,[5] but follow the judgment imprinted upon them by God. And since they do not cause their choice, they do not have freedom of choice.

Man, however, judging about his actions through his power of reason, can judge concerning his choice insofar as he can know the nature of the end and of the means to the end, and, likewise, the relation and order of the one to the other. Man, therefore, is his own cause, not only in moving but also in judging. Hence he has free choice, as one is speaking of the free judgments as to whether to act or not.

Article II

Whether Brute Animals Possess Free Choice

REPLY: We must say that brute animals in no way possess free choice.

In support of this contention, one must realize that since three things are involved in our operation—namely, knowledge, appetite, and the operation itself—the whole nature of liberty depends upon the mode of knowledge.

Appetite follows knowledge, since appetite seeks only the good, which is proposed to it by a cognitive power. Sometimes, though, an appetite appears not to follow cognition. This happens because the judgment of cognition and the appetite are not taken with respect to the same thing. For appetite is concerned with a particular thing to be done, while a judgment of reason is sometimes concerned with something universal, which occasionally is contrary to the appetite. But a judgment about this particular thing to be done now can never be contrary to the appetite. Whoever wishes to fornicate, although he knows in general that fornication is evil, nevertheless judges that an act of fornication

---

[5] Aquinas is referring here to the operation of the estimative power by which brutes are aware, without any learning, that certain things are good or bad for them. See his *Summa Theologiae*, I, 78, 4c; *De An.*, q. *unica*, a. 13c; *De Veritate*, q. 14, a. 1 ad 9.

for him now is good, and chooses it under the aspect of being good. For no one acts intending to do evil, as Dionysius says.[6]

If nothing interferes, however, motion or operation follow the appetite. Therefore, if the judgment of the cognitive power is not in someone's power, but is determined by another, then neither will his appetite be in his power. Consequently, neither will its motion nor operation be in his power absolutely.

Moreover, judgment is within the power of one judging insofar as he can judge of his own judgment. For we can judge of whatever is in our power. Indeed to judge of one's own judgment belongs only to reason, which reflects upon its own act and knows the relations of things of which it judges and through which it judges. The root of all liberty, therefore, is found in reason. Hence, according as something is related to reason, so is it related to free choice.

Now reason is found fully and perfectly only in man, and so free choice is found fully in him alone.

Brutes, however, have a certain semblance of reason, insofar as they participate in a certain natural prudence, in accordance with the way an inferior nature in some way attains what belongs to a superior one. This similitude consists in their having an orderly judgment about certain things. This judgment, however, arises out of a natural estimation, and not from any deliberation, since they are ignorant of the rationale of their judgments.[7] Because their judgment is of this kind, it does not extend to all things as does the judgment of reason, but only to certain determinate things.

---

[6] St. Thomas thought, as did all the scholars of his day, that they were in possession of a work composed by the Dionysius converted by St. Paul in Athens (Acts of the Apostles 17:34). More recent scholarship has shown that this work was composed in the late fifth or early sixth century. Reference is to *On Divine Names*, IV, 20, in *Dionysius the Areopagite on the Divine Names and the Mystical Theology*, trans. C. E. Rolt (London: Macmillan, 1940), pp. 115 and 127.

[7] See above, note 5.

Likewise, they possess something similar to free choice inasmuch as they are able to do or not do one and the same thing in accordance with their judgment. Therefore they possess something close to a certain conditioned liberty. If they judge that they should act, they can act; if they do not so judge, they can abstain from acting.

Since their judgment is determined to one thing, it follows that their appetite and action are likewise determined to one thing. Accordingly, as Augustine holds in *De Genesi ad Litteram*,[8] they are moved by what they see; or, as Damascene contends,[9] they are affected by their passions, because they naturally judge according to such sights or passions. By necessity they are moved by the sight of something or by an aroused passion toward it to flee or pursue that thing, as a sheep necessarily becomes afraid and flees at the sight of a wolf, or as a dog, because of an aroused passion of anger, must bark and pursue something in order to do it harm.

Man, however, is not moved necessarily by things appearing to him or by aroused passions, since he can either accept or reject them. Therefore, man has free choice, but brutes do not.

Article III

Whether God Has Free Choice

REPLY: We must maintain that God has free choice, but that He, angels, and men have it in different ways.

That God has free choice is evident from the fact that

---

[8] St. Augustine, *De Genesi ad Litteram,* Bk. IX, Pt. 14 in *Corpus Scriptorum Ecclesiasticorum Latinorum,* Vol. XXVIII, p. 284.

[9] St. John Damascene (*ca.* 675–749), a Syrian theologian who spent his first fifty years in active secular life, but joined a monastery for the remainder of his life, devoting himself to theological speculation and writing. Reference here is to his *The Orthodox Faith,* in *The Fathers of the Church,* 41 vols. to date, R. J. Deferrari *et al.,* eds. (New York: Fathers of the Church, Inc., 1958), Bk. III, chap. 18 (Vol. XXXVII, pp. 320–321).

He has for His will an end which He naturally wills, that is, His own goodness.[10] He wills all other things as ordered to this end, but, speaking absolutely, He does not will them necessarily. As was shown in the preceding question,[11] His goodness needs these other things which are ordered to it only as a manifestation of it, which manifestation can be suitably made in many ways. Hence, the free judgment to will this or that is open to Him, as it is to us; because of this we must say that free choice is found in God, and similarly in angels. For whatever they will they do not will necessarily, but rather, they will it according to a free judgment, as we do.

Nevertheless, free choice as found in us, in angels, and in God is different, since what is posterior must be diversified if what is prior is diversified.

Now the faculty of free choice presupposes two things, namely, a nature and a cognitive power. The way nature is found in God is different from the way it is in men and angels. For divine nature is uncreated, and is its own act of existing and its own goodness.[12] Hence, there cannot be any deficiency in it as regards the act of existing or goodness. Human and angelic nature, however, is created and arises out of nothing. Hence, considered in itself, it can be defective. Accordingly God's free choice can in no way be turned to evil, whereas the free choice of men and angels, considered in what is natural to it, can be turned to evil. Cognition as found in man is different from cognition as found in God and in angels. For man's cognition is obscure, arriving at a knowledge of truth in a discursive way. Hence, he is subject to doubt and to difficulties of discerning and judging. As the

10 St. Thomas maintains that God knows Himself, and other things in the knowledge of Himself (*Summa Theologiae*, I, 14, 2c and 5c). Since to will or to love is dependent upon knowledge, the "object" of God's love is Himself (as end) and other things (as serving His end). See *Summa Theologiae*, I, 19, 2c; *Summa Contra Gentiles*, I, 55–57; *De Veritate*, q. 23, a. 4.

11 St. Thomas, *De Veritate*, q. 22, a. 4c.

12 On God's goodness, see St. Thomas, *Summa Theologiae*, I, q. 6, aa. 1–4.

Book of Wisdom, 9:14, says: "The cognitions of men are fearful and our providence uncertain." But in God, and in angels in their own way, there is a simple vision of truth without any discursiveness or inquiry; neither doubt nor difficulty in discerning or in judging occurs in them. Therefore, both God and angels choose readily, but man suffers difficulty in choosing because of his uncertainty and doubt.

In this way it is evident how the free choice of angels holds a middle place between that of God and man, and participates equally in both extremes.

Article IV

Whether Free Choice Is a Potency or Not

REPLY: It must be said that if the term "free choice" is taken strictly, it names an action, but through usage it has come to signify the principle of the action.

When we say that man has free choice we do not mean that he is actually judging freely, but rather that he has in him that by which he can judge freely. Accordingly, if this act of judging freely contained something which exceeded the power of its potency, then "free choice" would name either a habit or the potency perfected by a habit,[13] as being angry in a moderate way denotes something which exceeds the irascible power.[14] For the irascible power of itself cannot moderate the passion of anger, unless it is perfected by some habit, according to which the moderating influence of reason is impressed upon it. Now if a free judgment does not include within itself anything exceeding the power of its potency, then "free choice" will name only the potency absolutely. Thus being angry does not exceed the power of the irascible potency; hence its proper principle is the potency and not a habit.

[13] For Aquinas a habit is a quality of a power, perfecting it and its operation. See above, *On the Virtues in General*, art. I (p. 77).

[14] See above, *On the Virtues in General*, note 26 (p. 81).

Now it is evident that a judgment to which nothing is added does not exceed the power of its potency, inasmuch as it is the act of some power, namely reason,[15] operating through its proper nature without any added habit being required. Nor, moreover, does adding the term "freely" exceed the power of the potency. For something is said to happen freely, if it is in the power of the one acting. For anything to be in our power, it would be in us according to some potency, namely the will, and not according to some habit.

Free choice, therefore, does not name a habit but the power of will or reason, one indeed ordered to the other. Thus the act of choice proceeds from one of them as ordered to the other. This accords with the Philosopher, who states in Book Six of the *Ethics* [16] that choice is an intellective appetite or an appetitive intellect.

It is clear from this why certain men [17] are inclined to maintain that free will is a habit. Some hold this because free choice adds to will and reason a certain order of one to the other. This order, however, cannot have the nature of a habit, if the word is used as it is properly accepted, since a habit is a distinctive quality according to which a potency is inclined to act. On the other hand, others,[18] considering the facility with which we judge freely, said that free choice is a potency modified by a habit. Judging freely, however, does not exceed the nature of a potency, as we have just said.

---

[15] See above, *On the Virtues in General*, note 42 (p. 87).

[16] Aristotle, *Nicomachean Ethics* VI. 2, 1139b4.

[17] St. Bonaventure, *In II Sent.*, in *Omnia Opera*, 10 vols. (Quaracchi: St. Bonaventure College Press, 1882–1902), d. 25, a. 1, q. 4 (*QR* II, 601b–602ab).

[18] Alexander of Hales, *Summa Theologica* (Quaracchi: St. Bonaventure College Press, 1924–   ), I–II, no. 390 (*QR* III, p. 488).

Article V

Whether Free Choice Is One Power or Many

REPLY: It must be said that two considerations led certain men [19] to propose that free choice is many powers.

One consideration is that they saw that we can, through free choice, perform acts which involve all the powers. They proposed, therefore, that free choice is a quasi universal whole with respect to all the powers. But this cannot be, since then it would follow that there are in us many kinds of free choice on account of the multitude of powers. For many men are many animals.

Nor are we forced to accept what they said on the basis of the reason given. For all acts of the different potencies are related to free choice only through the medium of one act, namely, choosing. Accordingly, we are moved by free choice because by our free choice we choose to be moved. The same holds for all the other acts. Hence this does not show that free choice is many powers, but rather that one power, of itself, moves diverse powers.[20]

The other consideration which led some to propose a plurality of powers of free choice arises from their having seen the act of free choice that involves acts of diverse powers, namely, judgment, which belongs to reason, and appetition,[21] which belongs to the will. Hence, they said that free choice contains many powers, just as an integral whole [22] contains its parts.

19 On the basis of available evidence, the men to whom St. Thomas refers here are unknown. See O. Lottin, *Psychologie et Morale aux XIIe et XIIIe Siècles* (Louvain: Abbaye du Mont César, 1942–1949), I, 177, note 1.

20 On the relation of the lower to the higher powers, see St. Thomas, *Summa Theologiae*, I, 81, 3c; I–II, 17, 7c; *De Veritate*, q. 5, a. 4.

21 *Appetition:* The English language lacks a commonly-used word to designate all the various actions of the will, such as wishing, choosing, loving, etc. The word "appetition" comes closest to functioning this way, and here is used to name the tending, as opposed to the knowing, aspect of an act of choice.

22 *Integral whole:* see above, *On Being and Essence*, note 28 (p. 40).

This, however, is not possible. Since the act attributed to free choice is one special act—namely, choosing—it cannot proceed immediately from two potencies. Rather, it proceeds from one immediately and from the other mediately, inasmuch as what belongs to a prior power remains in the posterior power. Hence, it is true that free choice is one power.

Article VI

Whether Free Choice Is the Will or Another Power Distinct From the Will

REPLY: It must be said that certain men [23] hold that free choice is a third power distinct from will and reason, because they see that the act of free choice, which is choosing, is different from the act of the simple will and from the act of reason. For the act of reason consists solely in cognition, whereas the act of the will concerns itself with the good, which is an end. Free choice, however, concerns itself with a good that is a means to an end. Now since a good which is a means to an end is outside the nature of end, and the appetite for the good is outside the knowledge of the good, therefore these men contend that the will proceeds from reason in a certain natural order, and that a third power, free choice, proceeds from these two.

But this position is not at all acceptable. For an object and the aspect according to which it is an object [24] pertain to the same power, just as color and light pertain to sight. The whole nature of the desirability of a means as a means is the

[23] St. Albert the Great, or Albertus Magnus (1193 or 1206–1280), a theologian, scholar, and teacher at many European universities, including the University of Paris. He was very influential in introducing Aristotle in the European universities, especially the scientific treatises. Aquinas was one of his students. Reference here is to his *Summae et Creaturis*, in *Omnia Opera* (Paris: L. Vivès, 1896), Pt. II, q. 70, a. 2c and ad 1 (Vol. XXXV, pp. 571, 576).

[24] Technically the former object is called the material object; the latter, the formal object.

end. Hence, it is not possible for the tendency to an end to pertain to one power, and the tendency to a means to that end pertain to another power.

Nor does this difference between the desire for an end absolutely and the desire for the means in relation to the end demand a distinction of appetitive potencies. For the ordination of one to the other does not pertain to the appetite through itself, but through another, namely through reason, to which it belongs to order and compare.[25] Such a distinction cannot be a specific difference, constituting a species of appetite.

The Philosopher, in Book Seven of the *Ethics*,[26] seems to leave in doubt whether choosing is an act of reason or of will. He offers the supposition, however, that it is equally a function of both, saying that choice is either an appetitive intellect or an intellective appetite. In Book Three of the *Ethics*,[27] however, he declares that free choice is an appetite, defining it as the desire for that about which previous deliberation has been made. The very object demonstrates that this is true. For just as the virtuous good [28] and the pleasurable good, which have the character of end, are objects of the appetitive power, so too is the useful good, which is properly chosen.

Moreover, the position is evident from its name. Free choice, as it has been said in Article IV of this question, is a potency by which man is able to judge freely. However, what is said to be the principle of performing an act in a certain way need not be the principle of that act without qualification. Rather, it is signified in some way to be

[25] Reason orders in the sense of giving direction, or specifying the good; the will orders by giving a command in accordance with reason. Cf. above, note 22 (p. 129).

[26] The Latin text reads Book Seven of Aristotle's *Nicomachean Ethics*, but Aquinas is most probably referring, as he did above (see note 16), to *Nicomachean Ethics* VI. 2. 1139b4.

[27] Aristotle, *Nicomachean Ethics* III. 3, 1113a9–12.

[28] Borrowing from Aristotle (*Nicomachean Ethics* I. 1, 1094a2–3), Aquinas defines the good as that which all things desire (*Summa Theologiae*, I, 5, 1c). On the kinds of good, see his *Summa Theologiae*, I, 5, 6; II–II, 145, 3.

the principle of that act, as in the case of grammar. Just because grammar is said to be the science of speaking correctly, it is not thereby said to be the principle of speaking simply, for a man can speak without grammar. Rather it is said to be the principle of correctness in speech. Likewise the potency by which we judge freely is not to be understood as that by which we judge simply, which is reason, but rather as the potency which accounts for the liberty in judging, that is, the will.[29]

Hence, free choice is the will itself. However, free choice does not name the will absolutely, but in relation to one of its acts, that is, choice.

Article VII

Whether Any Creature Can Have Its Free Choice Naturally Confirmed in Good

REPLY: One must say that there is no creature, nor can there be any, whose free choice is naturally confirmed in good in the sense that this creature, through what is purely natural to it, could not sin.

The reason is as follows. From a defect in the principles of action follows a defect in the action itself. Therefore, if there is anything in which the principles of action could not be defective of themselves or be impeded by some extrinsic source, it would be impossible for the action of that thing to be deficient. This is evident in the motion of the celestial bodies.[30] But a deficiency in action is possible in those things in which the principles of action can be deficient or impeded. This is evident in generable and corruptible things, whose active principles suffer a defect by reason of their mutability. Hence, their actions are also subject to deficiency. It is for this

---

[29] See above, Introduction, pp. 117–120. For a complete treatment of the will, see *Summa Theologiae*, I, q. 82, *passim*. For a consideration of the subtle relationships between intellect and will, see *ibid.*, especially a. 4.

[30] It was traditional in the Middle Ages to consider the motion of heavenly bodies as perfect because of its orderly and regular character.

reason that sin frequently occurs in the operations of nature, as is evident in the birth of monsters. For sin, whether in natural, artificial, or voluntary things, is nothing other than a defect or lack of ordination in a proper action, that is, when something is done in a way in which it ought not be done, as Book Two of the *Physics* makes evident.[31]

A rational nature endowed with free choice, however, acts differently from every other nature. Every other nature is ordered to some particular good, and its actions are determined with respect to that good. A rational nature, however, is ordered to the good simply. Just as truth taken absolutely is the object of the intellect,[32] so good taken absolutely is the object of the will. Hence, the will extends itself to the universal principle itself of goods which no other appetite can attain. Because of this a rational creature is not determined in its actions, but is related to material actions in a certain indifferent manner.

Since every action proceeds from an agent according to a certain similitude,[33] as a hot thing heats, then if an agent is ordained in its action to some particular good, it is necessary that the character of that good be naturally and immutably present in such an agent if its action is to be naturally indefectable. For example, if immutable heat is naturally present in some body, that body will immutably heat something else.

Consequently, rational nature, which is ordered to the good absolutely through various actions, cannot possibly perform actions which are naturally lacking a defect in goodness, unless the character of the universal and perfect good is present to it naturally and immutably. This, however, is possible only for the divine nature. For God alone is pure

---

[31] Aristotle, *Physics* II. 8, 199a33–b4.

[32] See above, *On the Virtues in General,* note 100 (p. 108).

[33] St. Thomas is referring to a doctrine fundamental to his theory of causality. Every agent acts in accordance with its form, and hence produces something like itself. Action and effect, if there is one, are proportioned to the kind of being acting. See his *Summa Theologiae,* I, 4, 3c; 6, 1c; 19, 2c; *Summa Contra Gentiles,* I, 8, 29, 44, 49.

act, having no mixture of potency. Consequently, He is pure and absolute goodness. Any creature is a particular good, since its nature contains a mixture of potency. This mixture of potency occurs inasmuch as the creature is *ex nihilo*.[34] Consequently, God alone among those having rational natures has free choice that is naturally impeccable and confirmed in goodness. This is indeed impossible for a creature since it is *ex nihilo*, as Damascene [35] and Gregory of Nyssa [36] state. And Dionysius says, in Chapter Four, *On Divine Names*,[37] that the reason for evil is founded on the fact that a good is particular.

Article VIII

Whether the Free Choice of a Creature Can Be Confirmed in Goodness Through Some Gift of Grace

REPLY: It must be said that on this question Origen [38]

34 *Ex nihilo:* traditional Latin formula for "created out of nothing." Insofar as all finite beings are created (St. Thomas, *Summa Theologiae*, I, 45, 3–5), and insofar as there can be only one being who is infinite and perfect (*ibid.*, q. 4, a. 3), all creatures must be limited in being. The act of existing of any being is limited by its essence. The relation between the two is one of act to potency. Cf. above, *On Being and Essence*, chap. IV (pp. 51–58).

35 St. John Damascene, *The Orthodox Faith*, II, 27.

36 St. Thomas is referring here to a work entitled *De Natura Hominis* 41 (in *Patrologiae cursus completus, series graeca*, ed. J. P. Migne; 166 vols. [Paris: 1857–1866], Vol. 40, p. 773), by Nemesius (*fl. ca.* 350), philosopher and bishop of Emesa, Syria. This work, however, was attributed frequently in the Middle Ages to St. Gregory of Nyssa (*d.* 394). Cf. Gilson, *History of Christian Philosophy in the Middle Ages*, pp. 60–64.

37 Pseudo-Dionysius, *On Divine Names* I, 20 and 32, in *Dionysius the Areopagite on the Divine Names and the Mystical Theology*, trans. C. E. Rolt (London: Macmillan, 1940), pp. 115 and 127. Cf. St. Thomas, *In Librum Beati Dionysii de Divinis Nominibus Expositio* (Rome: Marietti, 1950), chap. IV, lect. 16, no. 507; lect. 22, nos. 586–587.

38 Origen (*ca.* 185–*ca.* 254), probably the most famous Christian theologian before Augustine. His attempts, however, to reconcile Christian teaching and Greek conceptions of the universe raised questions as to his orthodoxy. Reference here is to his *On First Principles*, in *The Writings of Origen*, trans. F. Crombie, "Ante-Nicene Christian Library" (Edinburgh: T. and T. Clark, 1869), I, 5, no. 5 (Vol. X, pp. 44–53).

was in error, for he held that the free choice of creatures could in no way be confirmed in goodness, not even among the blessed. He excluded Christ, however, because of His union with the Word.

Because of this error he was forced to maintain that the beatitude of the saints and angels is not perpetual, but must sometime come to an end. From this it follows that their beatitude is not genuine, since immutability and security are of the nature of beatitude. Because of this unsuitable conclusion his position must be completely rejected. Therefore, it must be said simply that free choice, through grace, can be confirmed in good. This is evident from the following.

The free choice of a creature cannot be naturally confirmed in goodness because its nature does not possess the character of the perfect and absolutely good, but of a certain particular good. Through grace,[39] however, free choice is united to the absolute and perfect good, namely, God. Hence, if the union is perfect so that God Himself is the total cause of the action of free choice,[40] a defection to evil is not possible. This indeed happens to some creatures, especially the blessed. This is evident as follows.

The will naturally tends to good as its object. That it sometimes tends to evil happens only because the evil is proposed to it under the aspect of goodness. For evil is involuntary, as Dionysius says in Chapter Four of *On Divine Names*.[41] Hence, there can be no sin in a movement of the will, that is, the will cannot desire evil, unless there pre-exists a defect in the cognitive power, through which the evil is proposed to the will as a good.

This defect in reason can occur in two ways: either by reason itself or through something extrinsic to reason.

It can occur in reason itself because, although it naturally

---

[39] See above, *On the Virtues in General,* note 71 (p. 97).

[40] Cf. St. Thomas, *Summa Theologiae,* I, 82, 1; *De Veritate,* q. 22, a. 5; *De Malo,* q. 6, a. *unica.*

[41] Pseudo-Dionysius, *On Divine Names,* IV, 32 (*Dionysius the Areopagite,* p. 127). Cf. St. Thomas, *In Librum Beati Dionysii de Divinis Nominibus Expositio,* chap. IV, lect. 22, nos. 584–586.

and immutably possesses a faultless knowledge of good in general, both the good which is an end and the good which is a means, it does not possess such knowledge of the good in particular. Concerning this it can err, as when it judges something to be an end which is not an end, or something to be useful for an end which indeed is not useful thus. Because of this the will naturally desires the good that is an end—namely, happiness in general—and similarly the good that is a means, for everyone naturally desires what is useful to him. The will sins, however, in seeking this or that end, or in choosing this or that useful thing.

On the other hand, reason is deficient through something extrinsic to it, when an act of reason is hampered by inferior powers which are moved intensely to something. Consequently reason does not clearly and firmly propose its judgment about the good to the will. For example, when someone has judged rightly about preserving chastity, he might very well choose contrary to chastity through an ardent desire for the pleasurable. On account of this, reason's judgment is fettered in a certain way by concupiscence, as the Philosopher says in the seventh book of the *Ethics*.[42]

Now both of these defects are totally lacking in the blessed, because of their union with God. For those who see the divine essence know that God Himself is the end to whom the greatest love is due. They know also all those things in particular, both those things united to Him and those things distinct from Him, since they know God not only in Himself but also insofar as He is the reason for all other things. Through the clarity of this knowledge their minds will be so strengthened that no motion of the inferior powers can arise except according to the rule of reason. Therefore, just as now we immutably desire the good in general, so the minds of the blessed immutably desire in particular the appropriate good.

In addition to the natural inclination of the will, they will possess perfect charity, totally binding them to God.

<hr />

42 Aristotle, *Nicomachean Ethics* VII. 3, 1147a25–b5.

Hence, in no way could they fall into sin; hence they will be confirmed through grace.

Article IX

Whether the Free Choice of Man in This Life Can Be Confirmed in Goodness

REPLY: We must say that anyone can be confirmed in goodness in two ways.

First, without qualification; that is, when one has within himself the adequate principle of his constancy such that he is in no way able to sin. In this way are the blessed confirmed in goodness, for the reason stated in the previous article.

Some are said to be confirmed in goodness in another way, that is, by having been given a certain gift of grace by which they are so inclined to goodness that they cannot be easily turned aside from it. Nonetheless, this gift does not so remove them from evil that, without the protection of divine providence,[43] they would be immune from sin. The immortality of Adam, who is held to be immortal, is spoken of in this way.[44] He could not have been completely protected from every exterior mortal threat, like the incision of a sword and things of that sort, by something intrinsic to himself. He was, rather, preserved from these things by divine providence. In this way some in the present state of life can be confirmed in goodness; but they cannot be confirmed according to the first way, as is evident from the following.

[43] For Aquinas, the notion of divine providence is extremely complex. Everything, in its being and its activity, is dependent upon God as its efficient cause. In other words, God creates, conserves things in being, and moves them to their actions. In moving them to definite actions God seeks a goal. This divine movement is referred to as divine governance. The plan according to which God carries out his designs is called divine providence. On God's influence on creatures' actions, see St. Thomas, *De Potentia*, q. 3, a. 7. On God's purpose in creation see *De Potentia*, q. 5, a. 3 ad 4, and *Summa Theologiae*, I, 44, 4. On God's providence, see *Summa Theologiae*, q. 22, aa. 1–4.

[44] On Adam's gifts, see St. Thomas, *Summa Theologiae*, I, 97, 1.

No one can be rendered completely impeccable except through the removal of all sources of sin. Sin originates either through an error of reason which is deceived in a particular instance concerning the end, good, or the means to it, both of which are naturally desired in general; or else through a judgment of reason which is hampered by some passion of the lower powers.

Moreover, although it can be granted to someone in this life that his reason, thanks to gifts of wisdom and counsel,[45] is completely incapable of error concerning the end, good, and the means in particular, nevertheless, that reason's judgment may never be hampered exceeds the present state of life. This claim is made for two reasons.

First and foremost, it is impossible for reason always to be in the act of right contemplation in this life, such that the purpose of all its works would be God. Second, in this present state the inferior powers cannot be so subordinated to reason that an act of reason can in no way be impeded by them, except in the Lord Jesus Christ who, at the same time, lived on earth and already possessed Him.

A man, however, can be so united to good through the grace of this life that he is able to sin only with the greatest difficulty inasmuch as the inferior powers are restrained by the infused virtues,[46] the will is very strongly inclined to God, and reason is perfected in the contemplation of divine truth, the continuation of which, arising from the fervor of love, removes man from sin. But among those said to be confirmed, everything lacking for confirmation is supplied by the protection of divine providence, so that whenever an occasion of sin arises, their minds would be divinely inspired to resist.

[45] Wisdom and counsel are two of the seven gifts of the Holy Spirit. The other five are understanding, knowledge, fortitude, piety, and fear of the Lord (Isaias 11:2–3). St. Thomas compares the gifts to the moral virtues. See above, *On the Virtues in General*, *passim*. On the function of these gifts, see *Summa Theologiae*, I–II, 68, 3.

[46] See above, *On the Virtues in General*, art. X (pp. 99–102).

Article X

Whether the Free Choice of Any Creature
Can Be Obstinately Turned to, or Immutably
Confirmed in, Evil

REPLY: It must be said that on this question Origen erred.[47] For he contended that after a long time both demons and damned men would undergo a return to justice. He was moved, however, to propose this because of free choice.

This opinion indeed displeased all Catholic theologians, as Augustine says in the twenty-first book of *The City of God*,[48] not because they were hostile to salvation for the demons or the damned, but because it would be necessary to say, by a parallel reasoning, that the justice and glory of the beatified angels and men would likewise be terminated. Indeed, the glory of the good and the misery of the damned are simultaneously indicated as perpetual by St. Matthew, 25:46, where he says, "And these shall pass on to eternal punishment, and the just to eternal life." Even Origen seemed to understand this.

Wherefore it must be simply conceded that the free choice of the demons themselves is so confirmed in evil that it cannot possibly return to right willing.

To appreciate the reason for this latter position, one must understand how liberation from sin is caused. Two things enter into it: divine grace, which is the principal agent, and the human will, which cooperates with the grace. Accordingly Augustine says, "He who created you without you, will not justify you without you." [49]

47 Origen, *On First Principles*, I, 6 (Crombie, p. 56).
48 Augustine, *The City of God*, XXI, 17, in *Basic Writings of St. Augustine*, 2 vols., ed. and trans. Whitney J. Oates (New York: Random House, 1948), II, 587.
49 Augustine, Sermon 169, 11 (*PL*, XXXVIII, 923).

The cause of a confirmation in evil, therefore, must be taken partly from God and partly from free choice.

From God, but not as though He produces or conserves evil, but inasmuch as He does not offer His grace. His justice indeed demands this. For it is just that those who refused to choose well when they could, should be brought to the misery of not being able to choose well at all.

On the part of free choice, the cause of a reversibility or an irreversibility from sin must be understood in terms of those things by which a man falls into sin. Since there is naturally present in any creature an appetite for good, none can be induced to sin except under some form of an apparent good. For although a fornicator knows that fornication in general is evil, nonetheless, when he consents to fornication, he judges that fornicating is something good for him to do now.

Three things must be considered in a judgment like this. The first of these is the impetus of passion, viz., concupiscence or anger. Through it the judgment of reason is impaired, with the result that a man's actual particular judgment does not coincide with what he habitually knows in a universal way but follows the inclination of passion. Thus he consents to that toward which the passion tends as if it were something good in itself.

Secondly, there is the inclination of habit which indeed is like a certain nature for its possessor. The Philosopher says that custom is another nature; [50] and Cicero in his *Rhetoric* [51] says that virtue is in accord with reason after the manner of a nature, and likewise that a habit of vice is, as it were, a kind of nature which inclines one to what is suitable. Hence, anyone who has the habit of lust sees what is compatible with lust as something connatural. This is what the Philosopher

---

[50] Aristotle, *On Memory and Reminiscence* 2, 452a28.

[51] Marcus Tullius Cicero (106 B.C.–43 B.C.), the famous Roman orator, statesman, and philosopher. Reference is to his *De Inventione* II. 53, trans. H. M. Hubbell, "The Loeb Classical Library," No. 386 (Cambridge, Mass.: Harvard University Press, 1949), p. 327.

says in Book Three of the *Ethics:* [52] "An end will appear to someone in accordance with how he is interiorly."

The third of these is the false judgment of reason in its choice of something in particular. This follows either from the things we spoke about before, namely, the impetus of passion or the inclination of habit, or else from ignorance of a universal, for example, when someone erroneously thinks that fornication is not a sin.

Now against the first of these, free choice does have a remedy for renouncing sin. For he who is impelled by passion judges rightly concerning the end which is, as it were, a principle of those things which can be done, as the Philosopher says in the sixth book of the *Ethics*.[53] Hence, just as a man, through the true judgment that he has of the principle, can of himself reject any erroneous conclusions he may suffer, so too he can of himself reject every impetus of passion by being rightly disposed regarding the end. Hence, the Philosopher says in Book Seven of the *Ethics* [54] that "the incontinent man who sins because of passion can repent and is curable."

Similarly, free choice has a remedy against the inclination of habit. For no one habit corrupts all the potencies of the soul. Hence, despite the corruption of one potency by habit, there remains some rectitude in the other powers. Accordingly, man is induced to consider and to do those things opposed to that habit. For example, if someone's concupiscible power is corrupted by a habit of lust, he is incited by the irascible power to pursue something arduous, and the exercise of the irascible power removes the debilitating effects of lust. Thus the Philosopher states in *Categories* [55] that "the depraved man, having been led to better practices, will advance so as to become better."

Furthermore, free choice has a remedy against the third, namely, the false judgment of reason in its choice of something

---

[52] Aristotle, *Nicomachean Ethics* III, 5, 1114a33.
[53] *Ibid.,* VI. 5, 1140b16.
[54] *Ibid.,* VII. 8, 1150b30–33.
[55] Aristotle, *Categories* 10, 13a24–25.

particular. For whatever man accepts, he accepts, as it were, rationally—that is, through inquiry and comparison. Hence when reason errs about something, that error can be removed by contrary arguments, no matter what the source of the error might be. Accordingly, man is able to withdraw and desist from sin.

Angels are incapable of a sin of passion because, according to the Philosopher in Book Seven of the *Ethics*,[56] a passion is found only in a soul's sensible part, which angels do not possess. Hence only two things are relevant to the sin of angels, namely, a habitual inclination to sin and a false estimation of the cognitive power concerning some particular thing to be chosen.

Since angels do not possess a multiplicity of appetitive powers, as man does, whenever their appetite tends to something, it does so in a complete way; thus they have no inclination inducing them to the contrary.

Because they do not know in a rational way but, rather, in an intellective way,[57] whatever they judge they understand in an intellective fashion. Moreover, whatever is understood in an intellective fashion is understood irreversibly, as when anyone understands a whole to be greater than any of its parts. Angels, therefore, cannot reject their own judgment, once they have made it, whether it is true or false.

It follows from what has been said that the cause of the demons' confirmation in evil depends on three things, to which all the reasons assigned by theologians are reduced.

The first and foremost is divine justice. Accordingly, as a cause for their obstinacy, it has been assigned that since they did not fall through another, neither should they rise through another. Or if there is some other reason, it is of this kind, viz., that it pertains to the harmony of divine justice.

Secondly, there is the indivisibility of the appetitive power.

[56] Aristotle, *Nicomachean Ethics* VII. 3, 1147b16–17.

[57] Aquinas maintains here that angels do not know by inquiry and a reasoning process, but by immediate knowledge of the Divine Essence. See his *Summa Theologiae*, 1, 12, 10, ad 2; 74, 2c.

Accordingly, some claim that because an angel is simple, to whatever he commits himself, he commits himself completely. This must not be understood as a simplicity of essence, but as a simplicity which prohibits a division of powers of one kind.

Thirdly, there is intellectual cognition. For some say that the angels sinned irrevocably, inasmuch as they sinned against their intellect, which was like the divine.

Article XI

Whether Man's Free Choice in This Life Can Be Obstinate in Evil

REPLY: It must be said that obstinacy involves a certain stability in sin, because of which one cannot turn away from sin.

That someone cannot withdraw from sin can be understood in two ways.

First, that his powers are not capable of totally liberating him from sin. For example, it is said that anyone who falls into mortal sin is incapable of returning to justice. But no one is properly said to be obstinate because of this stability in sin.

In another way, that someone is so established in sin that he is incapable of cooperating so that he might rise again from sin. This, however, can be understood in two ways. First, he is incapable of cooperating in any way. This is perfect obstinacy, by which the demons are obstinate. For their minds are confirmed in evil to such an extent that every movement of their free choice is disordered and a sin. Therefore, in no way are they able to prepare themselves for receiving the grace through which their sin would be removed.

In another way, he is incapable of cooperating easily to remove himself from sin. This is imperfect obstinacy, by which anyone can be obstinate in this present state of life, as long as his will is so established in sin that he could make only weak attempts at goodness. Nevertheless, because some attempts do occur, these can be a way of preparing for grace.

The reason why a man in this state of life is incapable of being so obstinate in evil that he cannot cooperate in his liberation is evident from these facts: passion dissipates and is repressible; habit does not totally corrupt the soul; and reason does not adhere so pertinaciously to falsity that it is incapable of being changed by contrary reasoning.

But after this state of life the separated soul will not understand by receiving from the senses, nor will its appetitive powers of sense be in act.[58] Thus the separated soul is similar to an angel with respect to the mode of its understanding, and with respect to the indivisibility of its appetite, which were the causes of obstinacy in a fallen angel. Hence, for the same reason, the separated soul will be obstinate.

Finally, in the resurrection the body will follow the condition of the soul. The soul, therefore, will not return to the state in which it presently is, wherein it must learn through the body, although it will use bodily instruments.[59] Hence, the same cause for obstinacy will remain.

Article XII

Whether Anyone with Free Choice in the State of Mortal Sin Can Avoid Mortal Sin Without Grace

REPLY: It must be said that contrary heresies have arisen concerning this question.

[58] On the state of the soul after death, see St. Thomas, *Summa Theologiae*, I, 75, 5c.

[59] According to Aquinas, in this life, the body is not an instrument of the soul. St. Thomas sees man as a composite unit with soul and body related as form to matter; see above, *On Being and Essence*, chap. II (pp. 36–45). Aquinas, then, is contending in this section that the resurrected body will be related to the soul differently from the way it is in this life. The resurrected body will be completely subject to the soul and its will (*Summa Theologiae*, III, 54, 1 ad 2) and, hence, can be called the soul's instrument.

Certain men,[60] judging the nature of the human mind after the manner of corporeal natures, were of the opinion that man necessarily does all those things toward which the human mind seems inclined. From this they fell into contrary errors.

For the human mind has two contrary inclinations. One, indeed, is toward the good, through the natural instinct of reason. Considering this, Jovinian [61] said that man cannot sin. The other inclination is found in the human mind through the inferior powers, especially insofar as they are corrupted by original sin.[62] Accordingly, the mind is inclined to choose those things which are enjoyable to the carnal senses. Considering this inclination, the Manichaeans [63] held that man necessarily sins and in no way can avoid sin.

Thus both of these positions, although they arise from contrary approaches, are unsuitable for the same reason: they deny free choice. For if man is impelled necessarily either to good or to evil, he cannot then choose freely. The unacceptability of this can be proved by experience, by the doctrines of philosophers, and by the divine authorities, as is evident to some degree from what has been said previously.

---

60 Reference could be to any number of materialist philosophers. In his *De Malo* (q. 2, a. 9; q. 12, a. 1), St. Thomas indicates extensive aquaintance with the moral ideas of the Stoics, who held the view to which St. Thomas refers. See St. Justin Martyr, an early Christian who lived when the Stoics flourished, *The Second Apology of Justin* in *The Writings of Justin Martyr and Athenagoras,* trans. A. Roberts *et al.,* "Ante-Nicene Christian Library" (Edinburgh: T. and T. Clark, 1867), chap. VII (pp. 77–78).

61 Jovinian, an Italian of the late fourth century, who, because of his views on celibacy, fasting, and penance, was excommunicated in A.D. 388. A sect which championed his ideas caused both Augustine and Jerome (340?–420) to write in opposition. See, for example, St. Jerome, *Adversus Jovinianum,* in *Nicene and Post-Nicene Fathers,* Vol. VI, 2nd series (New York, 1893).

62 See St. Thomas, *Summa Theologiae,* I–II, 85, 3c; 1c; *De Malo,* q. 2, a. 11.

63 During the Middle Ages it was customary to refer to any doctrine of the dualism of good and evil as Manichaean. Originally the Manichaeans were followers of Mani (*ca.* 216–*ca.* 276), who eclectically adopted the teachings of many religions, but whose basic tenet was the goodness of the spirit and the evilness of matter.

Pelagius,[64] on the other hand, wishing to defend free choice but opposing divine grace, said that man can avoid sin without the grace of God. This error manifestly contradicts the doctrine of the Gospels and was therefore condemned by the Church.[65]

Catholic faith, on the other hand, follows a middle course, preserving freedom of choice without rejecting the necessity of grace.

As evidence for this it must be understood that since free choice is a certain power constituted under reason and over the consequent action, something is beyond the power of free choice in two ways. First, something exceeds the efficacy of the consequent action, which occurs at the command of free choice. Thus to fly is not within man's power of free choice, because it exceeds the ability of man's motor power. Second, something is beyond the power of free choice because of the fact that the act of reason does not extend to it. Since the act of free choice is an election following counsel—that is, the deliberation of reason—it follows that free choice cannot extend itself to what evades the deliberation of reason, like those things which occur without forethought.

In the first way, therefore, neither sin nor the avoidance of sin exceeds the power of free choice; for sin is accomplished in the will itself, through consent alone before the execution of the act, although the sin is completed by an exterior act in the execution of the motor power. Consequently, free choice is not impeded from sin or its avoidance because of a defect of the motor powers. It is sometimes impeded from executing the act, as when someone wills to kill, fornicate, or steal, but nevertheless cannot do so.

According to the second way, however, sin and the avoidance of sin can exceed the power of free choice, since some

[64] Pelagius (ca. 355–ca. 425), a celebrated monk and theologian, English by birth, who taught in Africa and Palestine in opposition to St. Augustine's conceptions of grace and predestination. He rejected the doctrine of original sin.

[65] Pelagianism was condemned by East and West at the Council of Ephesus (A.D. 431).

sins occur suddenly and take a person by surprise. They thus escape the election of free choice, although a person could freely choose to do or avoid them if he directed his attention or effort to them.

Now something can occur by surprise in us in two ways. First, from the impetus of passion; for example, a movement of anger or concupiscence sometimes prevents the deliberation of reason. Such a movement, tending to something illicit thanks to our corrupt nature, is a venial sin.[66]

Therefore, following upon the state of corrupt nature, it is not in the power of free choice to avoid all sins of this kind because they escape its act, although it can impede any one of these movements if it tries. However, it is impossible for a man to strive continually to avoid movements of this type, because of the mind's various preoccupations and because of the necessity for peace.

Indeed, this difficulty occurs because the inferior powers are not totally subject to reason as they were in the state of innocence, and when man found it very easy to avoid through free choice each and every sin of this kind, inasmuch as no motion could arise in the inferior powers except under the direction of reason. Generally speaking man is not in the present life, brought to this state of rectitude through grace. But we hope for this rectitude in the state of glory.[67] In this state of misery, therefore, and after his restoration by grace, man cannot avoid all venial sins, although this in no way compromises free choice.

Secondly, something can happen by surprise in us from the inclination of habit. Thus the Philosopher states in Book Three of the *Ethics:* "it is more courageous for those who are suddenly frightened to be fearless and unperturbed than for those who are forewarned."[68] The more an operation is due to habit, then, the less it is due to premeditation. When

---

[66] On venial sin, see St. Thomas, *Summa Theologiae*, I–II, 72, 5.

[67] On this state, see St. Thomas, *Summa Theologiae*, I–II, 3, 8; *De Veritate*, q. 8, a. 1; *Quodlibet*, 10, a. 8.

[68] Aristotle, *Nicomachean Ethics* III. 8, 1117a18–19.

someone is forewarned—that is, possessed of prior knowledge —his choice proceeds from reason and deliberation, not from habit. But the things that happen suddenly are chosen according to habit.

Nor should it be thought that the operation according to a virtuous habit can be completely devoid of deliberation since a virtue is an elective habit. But when someone has a habit, his end is already determined in his choice, therefore whenever anything occurs that is conducive to that end he immediately chooses it, unless he is impeded by something else that attracts his attention or by some greater deliberation.

But a man who is in mortal sin habitually adheres to sin. For although he may not always have the habit of a vice, inasmuch as no habit is generated from one act of lust, nevertheless the will of a sinner having forsaken the immutable good adheres to a mutable good as to an end. The strength and inclination of this adherence remains in the will until it again returns to the immutable good as to an end. Therefore, when it occurs to a man so disposed to do something which is in accordance with a prior choice, he will immediately tend to it through choice unless he be hindered himself by extensive deliberation. Nor is he excused from mortal sin by choosing this in such a rapid way, on the grounds that mortal sin requires a certain amount of deliberation. For that deliberation suffices for a mortal sin wherein one knows that what he chooses is a mortal sin and is against God.

Furthermore, this deliberation does not suffice to restrain him who is in mortal sin. For no one is restrained from doing that to which he is inclined unless it is proposed to him as being evil. But he who has already repudiated the immutable good for a mutable one does not now judge as evil this being turned from the immutable good, in which mortal sin essentially consists. Hence he is not restrained from sinning by adverting to the fact that something is a mortal sin. It is necessary further for his consideration to proceed to something which cannot be thought of except as being evil, such as unhappiness or the like. Therefore, before as much deliberation can occur as is required for a man so disposed to avoid mortal sin, consent to mortal sin takes place.

Accordingly, supposing an adherence of free choice to mortal sin or to an improper end, it is not in the power of free choice to avoid all mortal sin, although it can avoid any one sin, taken singly, if it resists. The reason is as follows. Although it will avoid this or that sin by using such deliberation as is required, nevertheless, it cannot do so without sometimes consenting to mortal sin prior to this deliberation, since it is impossible for a man always or for a long time to be in that state of vigilance necessary for such deliberation on account of the many things with which man's mind is occupied. Free choice can be removed from this disposition only through grace, through which alone the human mind is brought to adhere through charity to the immutable good as to an end.

From all the above, therefore, it is evident that we do not deny free choice, since we say that free choice is capable of avoiding or committing any sin taken singly; nor do we deny the necessity of grace, since we say that man cannot avoid all venial sin, although he can avoid individual ones. This is true even of the man who has grace, before that grace is perfected in the state of glory, because of the defect of our being incited. And when we say that man in the state of mortal sin and deprived of grace cannot avoid all mortal sin unless grace intervenes, although he can avoid singular sins, we do so because of the habitual adherence of his will to an inordinate end, which Augustine [69] compares to a curvature of the lower leg, from which a limp necessarily follows. In this way the opinions of the doctors, which appear different, are reconciled.

Some of these [70] claim that a man can avoid mortal sin without habitual grace, although he needs divine help, inasmuch as through His providence God leads a man to do good

---

[69] Augustine, *De Perfectione Justorum,* II, par. 4 (*Corpus Scriptorum,* XLII, 5–6).

[70] St. Bonaventure, *In II Sent.*, d. 28, q. 2, a. 2 ad 6 (*QR*, II, 687a); St. Albert the Great, *In II Sent.*, d. 24, a. 6 ad 2 (Vivès, Vol. 27, p. 403).

and avoid evil. This is true, though, only if a man desires to try to avoid sin; and in this way single sins can be avoided.

Others,[71] indeed, hold that a man without grace cannot avoid mortal sin for very long. This is also true, at least to the extent that a man habitually disposed to sin cannot live for a long time without having something mortally sinful suddenly occurring to him to which, because of his habitual inclination to evil, he consents. This follows from man's inability to exercise for a long time that solicitude which is necessary to avoid mortal sin.

Therefore, since each position in its own way forms both true and false conclusions, each has required a reply.

Article XIII

Whether Anyone Possessing Grace Can Avoid Mortal Sin

REPLY: We must say that there is a distinction between being able to abstain from sin and being able to persevere up to the end of life in abstaining from sin.

For when it is said that someone can abstain from sin, this implies a power over its negation only, namely, a power such that a person is capable of not sinning. This is possible for anyone possessing grace, speaking of mortal sin, because for him who possesses grace there is no habitual inclination to sin. Rather he possesses an habitual inclination to avoid sin. Hence, when something mortally sinful presents itself, he rejects it by this habitual inclination, unless he is inclined to the contrary through concupiscence. However, there is no necessity that he follow concupiscence, although he cannot avoid it when some movement of concupiscence arises which totally precedes the act of free choice. Therefore, since it is impossible not to have some movement of concupiscence totally preced-

[71] For example, St. Gregory the Great, *Morals on the Book of Job* (Oxford: J. H. Parker, 1845), Bk. XXV, chap. 9; St. Bonaventure, *In II Sent.*, 28, 2, 2, c (*QR* II, 686ab).

ing the act of free choice, it is impossible to avoid all venial sins. But, since no movement of free choice is ever placed without full deliberation, drawing him to sin as by the inclination of a habit, it is, therefore, possible to avoid all mortal sin.

On the other hand, when it is said that man can persevere up to the end of his life without sinning, such a capacity implies something affirmative such that someone constitutes himself in such a state that sin for him is an impossibility. For a man through an act of free choice can make himself persevere in no way other than by rendering himself impeccable. This, however, does not fall under the power of free choice, because the motive and executive power does not extend itself to this. Therefore, man cannot be for himself the cause of his perseverance, but must seek perseverance from God.

Article XIV

Whether Free Choice Can Accomplish Any Good Without Grace

REPLY: We must say that nothing acts beyond its species; rather, each thing is capable of acting according to the exigency of its species, inasmuch as nothing is deprived of its proper action.

Good, however, is twofold: there is a certain good which is proportioned to human nature, and another which exceeds the faculty of human nature.

These two goods, if we are speaking of actions, do not differ with respect to the substance of the act, but according to the mode of activity. For example, the act of giving alms is a good proportioned to human powers according as a man is moved by a certain natural love or generosity. However, according as man is induced to it out of charity,[72] which

72 See above, *On the Virtues in General,* note 105 (p. 110).

unites the mind of man to God, it exceeds the faculty of human nature.

Therefore, free choice without grace remains incapable of accomplishing that good which is beyond human nature. This is so because through a good of this sort a man merits eternal life, and without grace man cannot merit. Man is, however, capable of accomplishing through free choice that good which is proportioned to human nature. As Augustine says,[73] man is able through free choice to till the soil, build a house, and do many other good things without the operation of grace. However, although a man can perform good acts of this sort without grace, he cannot perform them without God. For nothing can perform its natural operations except through divine power, for a secondary cause cannot act except through the power of the first cause, as it is stated in the *Book on Causes*.[74] This is true of both those agents which act naturally [75] and those which act voluntarily. However, the necessity in both is of a different mode.

God is the cause of natural operation, inasmuch as He gives and conserves the intrinsic principle of the natural operation, from which a determined operation follows of necessity. For example, in the earth He conserves heaviness, which is the principle of downward motion. Man's will, however, is not determined to any one operation, but is related indifferently to many.[76] Thus it is in a certain way in potency unless moved by something active, which can be either something represented to it from without as an apprehended good, or something which affects it from within, as God himself.[77] Augustine speaks in this way in his book *On Grace and Free*

[73] Augustine, *Hypognos*, III, 4 (*PL*, 45, 1623).

[74] O. Bardenhewer, *Die pseudo-aristotelische Schrift . . .* , I, 163. See *On Being and Essence*, note 55 (p. 52).

[75] Cf. above, *The Principles of Nature*, pp. 15–16.

[76] See above, p. 133.

[77] For a full discussion of this problem, see St. Thomas, *De Malo*, q. 6, a. *unica*. Cf. Joseph Owens, *An Elementary Christian Metaphysics* (Milwaukee: Bruce, 1962), pp. 360–363; Gerard Smith, *Natural Theology* (New York: Macmillan, 1951), pp. 273–277.

Choice,[78] showing in many ways that God operates in the hearts of men. All external motions, too, are regulated by divine providence, which judges that someone should be excited to good by these or those actions.

Accordingly, if we wish to speak of the grace of God, not as some habitual gift but as the very mercy of God through which He interiorly affects the movement of the mind and orders exterior actions for man's salvation, then man can accomplish no good without the grace of God. Commonly speaking, however, we use the name "grace" for a certain habitual justifying gift.[79]

So it is evident that both positions conclude in a certain way to something false, and therefore have required a reply.

Article XV

Whether a Man Without Grace Can Prepare Himself to Possess Grace

REPLY: We must say that certain people [80] claim that man cannot prepare himself to possess grace, except by a certain grace freely given.

If by "grace freely given" they mean a certain habitual gift of grace, this opinion does not appear to be true, and for two reasons.

First, because a preparation for grace is said to be necessary in order that some reason be shown on our part why some receive grace and some do not. But if the very preparation for grace cannot occur without habitual grace, then either this habitual grace is given to all, or it is not. If it is given to all, it does not appear to be anything other than

---

[78] Augustine, *De Gratia et Libero Arbitrio,* 21 (*Patriologiae Series Latina,* 44, 908–909).

[79] On grace, see St. Thomas, *Summa Contra Gentiles,* III, 150 and 156; *Summa Theologiae,* I–II, 110, 3c and ad 3; 112, 1c; *ibid.,* 114, 3c; III, 62, 1c; *De Veritate,* 27, 2 ad 7.

[80] Bonaventure, *In II Sent.,* d. 28, a. 1c and ad 5 (*QR* II, 682a–683b).

a natural gift. For all men agree only in something which is natural. But natural things can be called graces insofar as they are given by God to man without any prior merits. If, on the other hand, it is not given to all, it will be necessary again to come back to the preparation and, for the same reason, posit some other grace, and so on to infinity. The first alternative is preferable.

Second, because preparing oneself for grace is the same as saying "doing what one can" just as it is commonly said that if a man does what he can, God gives him grace. Doing what one can is doing what is in one's power. Hence, if a man through free choice cannot prepare himself for grace, doing what he can will not be preparing himself for grace.

If, however, by "grace freely given" we understand divine providence, by which man is mercifully directed to the good, then it is true that without grace man cannot prepare himself to possess the grace which makes him worthy of possessing grace.

Two reasons make this evident.

First, because it is impossible for man to begin anything anew unless something moves him. This is evident from the Philosopher's remarks in Book Eight of the *Physics*,[81] wherein he maintains that the movement of animals following a period of quiet is necessarily preceded by some other motions by which the soul is aroused to action. And so, when man begins to prepare himself for grace by turning his will anew to God, he must be inspired to this by some exterior actions, like an exterior admonition, a corporeal illness, or by something similar. Or he may be moved by some interior instinct, according as God works in the minds of men. It may even be in both ways. All these, however, are provided man by divine mercy. Man, therefore, prepares himself for divine grace through divine mercy.

Second, because not just any motion of the will is a sufficient preparation for grace, just as not every sorrow is sufficient for the remission of sin; rather some determinate mode is re-

[81] Aristotle, *Physics* VIII. 2, 253a11–21.

quired. This mode, indeed, man cannot know since the very gift of grace exceeds man's cognition, inasmuch as it is impossible to know the mode of preparation for a form, unless the form itself be known. Moreover, whenever some definite mode of operation unknown to the operator is required to do something, the operator needs guidance and direction. It grace, unless it is divinely directed to it.

For these two reasons God is asked in Scripture in two ways to bring about this preparation for grace in us. One way asks that He convert us to Himself from that to which we have wandered. This is for the first reason, as when it is said, "Convert us, God, our salvation." [82] The second way asks that He guide us, as when it is said, "Guide me in your truth." [83] This is for the second reason.

[82] Psalms, 84:5.
[83] Psalms, 24:5.

Index